Negotiating Critical Literacies with Young Children

"Through vibrant, memorable, and surprising examples of very young children grappling with very real social issues, Vivian Maria Vasquez has transformed critical literacy in early childhood education."
Karen Wohlwend, Indiana University-Bloomington, USA

"These amazing accounts, supplemented with advice for implementing critical literacy practices with young children, will inspire many teachers to explore the potential of their students' voices and the power of young children to work for change in their schools and communities."
Catherine Compton-Lilly, University of Wisconsin Madison, USA

"Vasquez' book provides sound critical theory and an abundance of practical examples of young children asking sophisticated questions about the texts of their lives, from McDonald's to TV to their own school community."
Stephanie A. Flores-Koulish, Loyola University MD, USA

"This is a brilliant, essential, uplifting, and inspiring book needed more now than ever."
Doug Morris, Eastern New Mexico University, USA

"The critical and creative ways of being in Vivian's preschool classroom should be a model of living and learning for all of us."
Stephanie Jones, University of Georgia, USA

"Dr. Vasquez is a pioneer in developing and sharing how to develop critical classroom practices."
Carmen L. Medina, Indiana University, USA

"A concise and practical book that opens up doors for pedagogical possibilities in literacy classrooms."
Korina Jocson, Washington University in St. Louis, USA

"Vivian Vasquez's groundbreaking work is essential reading for early childhood literacy teachers and scholars."
María Paula Ghiso, Teachers College, Columbia University, USA

"This is a cornerstone book for educators who work with young children."
Bobbie Kabuto, Queens College, City University of New York, USA

Vivian Maria Vasquez is Professor, American University, School of Education, Teaching and Health, USA.

Language, Culture, and Teaching
Sonia Nieto, Series Editor

Visit **www.routledge.com/education** for additional information on titles in the **Language, Culture, and Teaching** series.

Negotiating Critical Literacies with Young Children

10th Anniversary Edition

VIVIAN MARIA VASQUEZ

Routledge
Taylor & Francis Group

NEW YORK AND LONDON

The drawing on the cover of the book was created for an award-winning book-
mark a group of 4-year-old girls submitted to a contest on International Women's
Day. It includes the girls' interpretation of "women and girls being strong."

This Edition published 2014
by Routledge
711 Third Avenue, New York, NY 10017

and by Routledge
2 Park Square, Milton Park, Abingdon, Oxon OX14 4RN

*Routledge is an imprint of the Taylor & Francis Group, an informa
business*

© 2014 Taylor & Francis

First Published 2004 by Lawrence Erlbaum Associates

Library of Congress Cataloging-in-Publication Data

Vasquez, Vivian Maria.
  Negotiating critical literacies with young children : 10th anniversary
edition / Vivian Maria Vasquez. — Second edition.
    pages cm. — (Language, culture, and teaching series)
  Includes bibliographical references and index.
 1. Language arts (Early childhood)—Social aspects—United
States. 2. Language arts (Early childhood)—Curricula—United
States. 3. Critical pedagogy—United States. I. Title.
  LB1139.5.L35V37   2014
  372.6—dc23   2013033520

ISBN: 978-0-415-73316-8 (hbk)
ISBN: 978-0-415-73317-5 (pbk)
ISBN: 978-1-315-84862-4 (ebk)

Typeset in Dutch823BT
by Apex CoVantage, LLC

Printed and bound in the United States of America by Sheridan Books, Inc. (a Sheridan Group Company).

To TJ and Andy, now and forever . . .

◼ *Contents*

Preface

As a public school teacher, I was introduced to critical literacy in the mid-1990s. At the time, I was taking a course through Mount Saint Vincent University that was being held at the University of South Australia. Until that time, I believed the whole-language movement (e.g., Goodman, Watson, & Burke, 1987; Harste, Short, & Burke, 1996; Harste, Woodward, & Burke, 1984) seemed to be the most generative theoretical position from which to support the needs of learners. Whole language gave me a way of envisioning and supporting learning as a social experience, of creating spaces in classrooms for placing children at the center of pedagogy, and of framing my teaching from an inquiry perspective to ensure that my students' interests were foregrounded.

Whole language, however, is not static. As my understanding grew and I encountered new experiences and participated in new discourse communities, I found myself taking on a more critical position. The journey toward critical literacy was rooted in my early experience as a literacy learner.

I remember being a kindergarten student. It was Friday morning, the last day of the week, the day when all our efforts as kindergarten students were rewarded. I was 5 years old. One day, I walked into my classroom at the sound of the school bell and found one black sheet of construction paper, one green piece of construction paper, one square piece of yellow paper, one red circle, scissors, and a bottle of glue, neatly organized across the desk I shared with another 5-year-old. I took the red circle, traced it onto the black sheet of paper, and proceeded to cut carefully along the line I had drawn. "Stop! Is that what I told you to do? You are doing it all wrong. It took me a long time to get all this organized and now look at what you've done!" My teacher's voice echoed in my head. Suddenly I wanted to be anywhere but in that classroom. I wanted to be anywhere far away from there. I remember having to struggle to see the circles I held tightly in my hand. The tears that welled in my eyes streamed down my cheeks and blurred my vision. I remember watching the teacher hang my classmates' stoplights on the classroom bulletin board while my efforts lay crumpled in the garbage can where my teacher had thrown it. To this day—I remember.

At the end of the day, each child in the class was given a small card with an angel printed on it. There was a yellow angel, a purple angel, a green angel, and a blue angel. There was also a gold angel that everyone wanted because it symbolized excellent work and effort throughout the week. Then there was the black angel, on a white card. It was most undesirable because the black angel represented the angel who fell from God's grace. On this day, only two kinds of cards were handed out, 30 gold angels and one black angel. I had fallen from grace. Humility became my punishment as my teacher used me as an example of what would happen to those children who do not listen to instructions carefully, those children who choose not to conform, or those children who think for themselves and make decisions on their own without first asking for the teacher's approval. Anyone who strayed from the teacher's direct instruction, whether deliberate or not, would face the same fate.

As a young immigrant child, female, and a member of an underrepresented minority, I frequently found my identity was constructed and maintained as voiceless, as incapable of action, of making a difference in the lives of others, or indeed, in my own life. I was born in the Philippines, the oldest of four children, and was in elementary school when my family left the islands in search of a better life in North America. Before I set foot in a North American school, my parents and other relatives told me about the rules of school. Basically, these were the same rules that I had learned from being raised Catholic: always respecting your elders. Catholicism is widespread in the Philippine Islands and my family were devoted Catholics. As a child growing up in a religious household, I was taught to do as I was told and to accept the consequences if I did otherwise. When I inadvertently disobeyed my teacher as a result of misunderstanding what she had expected of me, the only response I knew was to accept my punishment.

At first glance, my black angel story may seem mundane, but the discourse of controlling *what, how,* and *when* children learn, as well as *who* gets to learn *what,* continues to exist even though there have been many gains at constructing more equitable schooling. Unfortunately, the scale continues to be tilted in favor of dominant cultural ways of being, leaving children such as the immigrant children described by Igoa (1995) at a disadvantage. According to Igoa, "When immigrant children leave the country that was their home—a familiar language, culture, and social system—they experience a variety of emotional and cognitive adjustments to the reality of life in a new country" (p. xi). I feel as though Igoa was writing about me as her words certainly describe my experience.

A discourse of control, which I lived as a young child at school, can be found through artifacts of schooling such as mandated common core curriculum, standardization, and high-stakes testing. The stoplight craft that I did incorrectly, for example, was part of a pre-packaged curriculum that dictated what should be "covered" and when and how those things should be done. But this is not only a personal experience; much of what takes place in schools and in communities where I grew up, in North America, is inaccessible to certain marginalized groups, including immigrant children, especially those who are people of color, because of the way in which curriculum is often developed from the top down, from administrators in distant school district offices who are not in touch with the children or the day-to-day living in schools they are meant to support.

A critical perspective suggests that deliberate attempts to disrupt inequity in the classroom and society need to become part of our everyday classroom life. For me, this meant that I needed to construct a critical curriculum that was socially just and equitable, where social issues such as culture, class, gender, fairness, and ability were constantly on the agenda and where diverse children's questions were given importance and used in building curriculum. This is the start of negotiating a critical literacy curriculum with children.

Nothing Is Significant Until You Make It Significant

I once watched a television interview with the author Frank McCourt. The interviewer asked him how he knew what incidents in his life to make important for inclusion in his book *Angela's Ashes* (McCourt, 1996). McCourt replied by saying that nothing is significant until you make it significant. The kind of curriculum I have in mind is one that cannot be prepackaged or preplanned. It is the kind of curriculum that deliberately "makes significant" diverse children's cultural and social questions about everyday life. It arises as teachers and children tune in to issues of social justice and equity that unfold through classroom discussion and begin to pose critical questions such as:

- What is this text trying to do to me?
- Who is marginalized or privileged by this text?
- Whose account of a particular topic or issue is missing? Said differently, whose voices are silenced?
- Whose voices are dominant?
- Whose reality is presented?
- Whose reality is ignored?

Discussions like these include underlying questions such as:

- In what ways are we already readers, writers, and analysts of the world?
- In what ways can we equitably and democratically reread and rewrite the world in order to become the literate people we want to be?
- How do texts work to create certain subject positions or ways of acting and thinking, and what discourses maintain these ways of being?
- What discourses maintain certain social practices and cultural models? For what purpose? To whose advantage?

These kinds of questions and discussions are central to my work and to this book. What I offer is not a specific way of doing critical literacy. Jenny O'Brien (2001, p. 37) said it best when she stated,

> This is how the particular critical positions which I introduced in [the classroom] worked for my students and for me; these are the circumstances in which I introduced critically framed activities and talk; these are the personal and institutional histories that were associated with their introduction; and, several years later, this is how I now reread what happened.

In this book, I show and tell what happened as my 3- to 5-year-old students and I seized opportunities to use everyday issues and everyday texts drawn from our school, community, and the children's personal inquiries and questions to negotiate a critical literacy curriculum over the course of a school year. To this end, throughout the book, I describe how my students and I negotiated a critical literacy curriculum; show how we dealt with particular social and cultural issues and themes; and share the insights I gained as I attempted to understand what it means to frame my teaching from a critical literacy perspective. My hope is that you will be able to create spaces in your setting from the stories in this book to intersect with your teaching and inform the work you do in the classroom.

Negotiating Critical Literacies with Young Children is written from the perspective of an early-childhood teacher-researcher. However, it is intended for all interested readers concerned with issues of social justice and equity in school settings and the political nature of education, along with those interested in finding ways to make their curriculum critical. From this perspective, there is something to be learned from the teaching practice shared in the book whether you work with younger children or older children.

Acknowledgements

I sincerely thank Naomi Silverman, my editor, and Sonia Nieto, my series editor. Their respect for my work, encouragement, and vision gave me the confidence to write the original edition of this book. Nine years later, Naomi enthusiastically approached me with the idea of doing a 10th anniversary edition. For many reasons, her timing was perfect, and I am thrilled to have had yet another opportunity to do another project with her. Naomi has not only been my editor but I consider her to be one of my mentors: someone who has nurtured my scholarly life. Best of all, through the years, she has become a friend who has held an important place in my life. I also extend much thanks to Christina Chronister, Editorial Assistant at Routledge, for her work on the book and in particular for her attention to detail and to Denise File and the folks at Apex CoVantage for preparing the final manuscript. Thank you to Catherine Compton-Lilly, University of Wisconsin Madison; Carole Edelsky, Arizona State University (Emerita); Maria Paula Ghiso, Teachers College, Columbia University; Korina Jocson, Washington University in St. Louis; Stephanie Jones, University of Georgia; Bobbie Kabuto, Queens College, City University of New York; Mitzi Lewison, Indiana University; Carmen L. Medina, Indiana University; Doug Morris, Eastern New Mexico University; and Karen Wohlwend, Indiana University-Bloomington for their thorough and thoughtful reviews, suggestions, and endorsements.

Jerry Harste, Barbara Comber, Andy Manning, Allan Luke, and Hilary Janks have pushed my thinking for more than 20 years. I am indebted to them for their ongoing support, belief, and trust in my work and in me as a person. I have learned more than I can imagine in their company.

Judith Newman, June Gravel, and Marilyn Cerar were voices from my past who first told me that my stories were important. Thank you for encouraging me to write them down. My Indiana University family, especially my guardian angel Dorothy Menosky and my colleagues-turned-friends, Carolyn Burke, Ginny Woodward, and Jan Harste, welcomed me from the start, as I began doctoral studies and played with the data that led to this book. They helped make Bloomington, Indiana, feel like home.

Since the initial book was published, I have heard from numerous people from around the world who have shared how this work has informed their thinking. You know who you are. There are too many names to include here, but I do sincerely thank you for taking the time to connect with me. Gerald Campano, Denny Taylor, Carmen Medina, Karen Wohlwend, Anne Haas Dyson, and Jackie Marsh, we don't connect with each other often enough, but your consistent and ongoing kindness and support through the years are greatly appreciated.

To my DC area colleagues and friends, especially Carol Felderman, Stacie Tate, Brec Cooke, Alex Hodges, and Sarah Irvine-Belson— Thank you!

Of course, I would like to acknowledge the children and their families for being so engaged and supportive of critical literacies during our time together and those of you who have breathed life into this book through your support of the first edition. Thank you.

Finally, I thank my family, Reggie Sr., Lily, Vickie, Reggie Jr., Victor, Nanay, Jim Clohessy, Paz Mayoral, and Diane Marlatt for always believing I could do what I set my mind to and for reading my writing even when it didn't always make sense. I am glad I was born into our family.

My life partner and best friend, Andy Bilodeau, has supported my efforts and the decisions I have made for almost 30 years, even when it meant moving away from his family and friends; for this and for keeping the home fires burning as I moved from one project to the next and helping with my tech needs throughout, I am eternally grateful. Thank you for having my back even during the times when I have had to roll a hard six. Finally to my TJ—you make each morning brighter, and above all, being your mom brings me more joy and happiness than I could ever imagine.

—*Vivian Maria Vasquez*

Special Thanks

I would like to extend my gratitude to Faige Meller and Minda Morren Lopez who shared their audit trail/learning wall stories for inclusion in this book. I know your work will inspire others as it has inspired me.

Introduction

Living a Critical Literacy Curriculum

A critical literacy curriculum needs to be lived. It arises from the social and political conditions that unfold in communities in which we live. As such, it cannot be traditionally taught. Furthermore, as teachers, we need to incorporate a critical perspective into our everyday lives (Vasquez, Tate, & Harste, 2013) in order to find ways to help children understand and act upon the social and political issues around them. As hooks (1994) reminds us, teaching should be the kind of work that engages not only the student but also the teacher. Incorporating a critical perspective into our everyday lives as teachers is therefore about living critical literacies by experiencing firsthand what it would mean to take on this perspective as a way of framing our participation in the world. This kind of experience helps us to better understand what it would take to create spaces for critical literacy in the early-years classroom. Resource Box I.1 includes a list of texts focused on living critical literacies as adult learners.

Working from a critical perspective, my desire is to construct spaces where social justice and equity issues can be raised and a critical literacy curriculum can be negotiated with children. Critical literacy makes it possible for me to reconsider my thinking by providing a framework or theoretical perspective from which to address social issues such as gender, race, class, and age. I imagine critical inquiry, negotiation, contestation, and reimagination at the center of these discussions rather than a more familiar process of discovering

1

Resource Box I.1 Resources on Living Critical Literacies

Rogers, R. (2013). Cultivating Diversity Through Critical Literacy in Teacher Education. In Kosnik,C., Rowsell, J., Williamson, P., Simon,R., and Beck, C. (Eds) *Literacy Teacher Educators: Preparing Teachers for a Changing World.* N.Y., N.Y.: Sense Publishers. pp. 7–20.

Rogers, R., Mosley, M., Kramer, MA (2009). *Designing Socially Just Learning Communities: Critical Literacy Education Across the Lifespan.* New York, N.Y.: Routledge.

Simon, R. (2013) Literacy Teacher Education as Critical Inquiry. In Kosnik, C., Rowsell, J., Williamson, P., Simon, R., and Beck, C. (Eds) *Literacy Teacher Educators: Preparing Teachers for a Changing World.* N.Y., N.Y.: Sense Publishers. pp. 121–134.

Vasquez, V.M., Tate, S.L., Harste, J.C. (2013). Negotiating Critical Literacies with Teachers: Theoretical Foundations and Pedagogical Resources for Pre-service and In-service Contexts. New York, N.Y.: Routledge.

Vasquez, V. (2013) Living and Learning Critical Literacy in the University Classroom. In Kosnik, C., Rowsell, J., Williamson, P., Simon,R., and Beck, C. (Eds) *Literacy Teacher Educators: Preparing Teachers for a Changing World.* N.Y., N.Y.: Sense Publishers. pp. 79–9.

---

the best way. Learning would therefore be a process of reimagining, adjusting, reconstructing, and redesigning what we know rather than of accumulating information, filling a blank slate, or covering a predetermined mandated or core curriculum.

Shortly, I propose to show and tell what happened when my 3- to 5-year-old students and I seized opportunities to use everyday issues and everyday texts from our school and community to negotiate a critical literacy curriculum over the course of a school year. To do this, I describe in detail and analyze a series of critical literacy incidents that took place in our classroom. There were many critical incidents that happened throughout the year. There were too many to have included them all in one book. One of the questions I am often asked is how I decided which incidents to include. The process for choosing which incidents to elaborate was simple. I had three primary objectives: (1) I wanted to make visible teaching practices that were varied in scope; (2) I wanted to address different issues and topics and the different ways we took up those issues and topics; and (3) I wanted to include topics or interests shared by other educators in order to maximize the ways in which this book might impact their work.

Regardless of the context in which we teach, we all make choices regarding what topics to take up in our classrooms. Authors and researchers make these choices all the time when working with data and writing up their data. Our choices are never innocent. The important question to ask ourselves is what perspectives, ideologies, and discourses underlie those choices. There will be topics that will inevitably rise to the surface and others that will remain untouched. What we make central to our curriculum depends on our intent for choosing particular topics or issues. What are our motivations? What literacies are we attempting to produce and for what purpose? Asking ourselves how we decide on what issues to take up in our classrooms and what is the theoretical context in which we make those decisions is a powerful way of making visible the perspectives from which we do what we do in the classroom. Making these perspectives visible creates an opportunity for us to reflect on their effects for the purpose of potentially reimagining new ways of framing our teaching practice.

Before sharing a series of critical literacy incidents, I want to provide some context for talking about our experiences by sharing my current stance on critical literacy and what it means to me now and for the future and outlining briefly how I came about putting a critical literacy curriculum in place. I will also explain my use of an audit trail to document and analyze this curriculum as well as to initiate critical conversation with young children.

What Is Critical Literacy?

Critical literacy has been a topic of debate for quite some time. Much of this can be attributed to longstanding beliefs held by proponents of critical literacy (Comber & Simpson, 2001; Luke & Freebody, 2003; Vasquez, 2001, 2004) that it should look, feel, and sound different and accomplish different sorts of life work depending on the context in which it is being used, as a theoretical and pedagogical framework for teaching and learning (Comber & Simpson, 2001; Luke & Freebody 2003; Vasquez, 2001, 2004). I have referred to this framing as *a way of being*, where I have argued that critical literacy should not be an add-on but a frame or perspective through which to participate in the world both in and outside of school (Vasquez, 1994). Through this participation, students and teachers together are able to work toward disrupting problematic inequitable ways of being.

As such, critical literacies are not just about disrupting, critiquing, or thinking deeply about texts: They also need to be about the active production and redesign of those problematic ways of being. This involves figuring out how systems and institutions work to position people in advantageous or disadvantageous ways. Of central concern in this work is therefore unpacking the relationship between meaning systems (i.e., language, art, math) and power. These systems sometimes conflict and at other times are complimentary. It is therefore important to ask, what are the discourses that keep these systems in place? Once we know this, we can begin to disrupt those discursive practices and put alternate practices in place.

Critical Literacy Texts

Some authors have written about what they refer to as "critical literacy text." The problem is there is no such thing as a critical literacy text. However, all texts can be read from a critical perspective. As we do so, we can ask questions such as those listed earlier in the preface of this book:

- What is this text trying to do to me?
- Whose interests are marginalized or privileged by this text?
- Whose account of a particular topic or issue is missing? Said differently, whose voices are silenced?
- Whose voices are dominant?
- Whose reality is presented?
- Whose reality is ignored?
- What are the positions from which I am reading this text?
- What experiences am I drawing from to make meaning from this text?

Clearly, some of these questions may seem overly complex and complicated if working with very young children. One reason for writing this book is to make visible possibilities for addressing these sorts of questions with preschool or kindergarten-aged children. In the chapters that follow, you will read examples of what some of these questions look and sound like when 3–5-year-olds take on various social issues.

After asking and exploring such questions, we then need to consider alternates or redesigns of texts that we deem to be problematic. Although you will read examples of this throughout the book, following are some strategies that have been used as an introduction into doing this work:

- Comparing the language used in texts that are related in some way.
- Exploring text sets that consist of multiple books focused on the same topic that usually offer different takes on that topic. Sometimes these are conflicting texts.
- Reading different multimodal texts against one another.
- Unpacking the historical and cultural contexts of discourses in texts and images.

Which strategies you choose depends on close observation of the children and what you identify as topics or issues that are of interest to those children.

Building a Critical Literacy Curriculum

Building and negotiating a critical literacy curriculum begins with close observation of children not only in the classroom but also in such places as the school bus, or while walking down the hallway, and while playing in the schoolyard. These observations include tuning in to the things that bother them, the things that make them happy, the questions they ask, their worries, and their passions. Sometimes topics and issues of importance to children are ascribed on their bodies, the printed images on the clothes they wear, on their backpacks and shoes, and so forth. Observations of the children I describe in this book predominantly took the form of written anecdotes and gathering work they had produced, such as writing or art pieces that represented their learning. To record anecdotes, I made use of a chart based on Diane Stephens' (1999) hypothesis test form. The form was divided into four columns: observations/interpretations, hypothesis, curricular decisions, and reflections (Fig. I.1.). In the observations/ interpretations column, I noted my thoughts on what I saw children doing and saying. I did this at different points during the day. At the end of the day, I would look across my observations and interpretations looking for patterns and anomalies. Patterns and anomalies made up my jottings in the hypothesis column. Once having considered a number of hypotheses from different perspectives, I used the curricular decisions column as a planning-to-plan site for considering possible experiences and strategies to use with my students.

Observations/ Interpretations	Hypothesis	Curricular Decisions	Reflections

FIG. I.1.   Observation Chart.

The reflections column was filled out after my attempts to engage the curricular strategies I had previously outlined.

Creating Spaces for Critical Literacies

Opportunities for creating spaces to engage with critical literacies do not just happen. Opportunities arise as we create opportunities for children to first make visible what is on their minds. What this means is that the issues and topics of interest that capture learners' attention as they participate in the world around them can and should be used as text to build a curriculum that has significance in learners' lives and that is developmentally sensible. Following are key tenets that comprise a critical literacy perspective. These tenets are informed by the work of Luke and Freebody (1999) and their Four Resources Model; Janks' (2010) Interrelated Model for Critical Literacy; Comber's work on critical literacy in the early years (2001); and Marsh's work on new technologies (2005). This list is adapted from a previous publication on critical literacy and technology in early childhood settings (Vasquez & Felderman, 2013a):

- Critical literacy involves having a critical perspective or stance (Vasquez, 1994, 2004; Vasquez & Felderman, 2013a; Vasquez et al., 2013).
- Critical literacy is a perspective from which to engage in the day-to-day living in a classroom rather than as a unit of study that lasts for a predetermined amount of time (Vasquez & Felderman, 2013a).
- The children's funds of knowledge and diverse ways of practicing literacy should be privileged in the curriculum (Comber, 2001; Vasquez, 1998).
- The children's multimodal literacy practices should be utilized (Comber, 2001; Vasquez, 1998).
- The world is a socially constructed text that can be read (Frank, 2008). As such, when we read the word, we simultaneously read the world (Freire & Macedo, 1987).
- Texts are never neutral (Freebody & Luke, 1990). As such, all texts are socially constructed, meaning that someone from a particular standpoint, position, point of view, or stance has created that text. Therefore, there is nothing natural or normal about any text, whether it is a book or a text from everyday life such as an advertisement flyer or cereal box.
- Texts work to create particular subject positions that make it easier or harder for us to say and do certain things; therefore, we need to interrogate the perspective(s) presented through texts (Meacham, 2003). This means that texts are not only socially constructed; they are also socially constructive offering particular ways of being, doing, talking, and thinking that shift from context to context.
- We read from (a) particular subject position(s), so our readings of texts are never neutral, and we need to interrogate the position(s) from which we read (speak, act, do . . .). Just as no text is neutral, natural, or normal, our reading of a text is never neutral, natural, or normal either. Our readings of text are rooted in our discursive practices and the cultural models through which we live our lives (Vasquez & Felderman, 2013a, 2013b).
- What we claim to be true or real is always mediated through discourse (Gee, 1999). We can never speak outside of discourse.

As we engage with text or other people, we bring with us ways of being, doing, and thinking that help shape what we say and do (Vasquez & Felderman, 2013a).

- How we choose to teach, the decisions that we make, are political decisions (Janks, 2010). Understanding this is a first step in developing political awareness that helps us to better unpack why things are the way they are and how things could be different.
- Critical literacy practices can contribute to change (Freebody & Luke, 1990; Freire & Macedo, 1987; Vasquez, 2004). This builds on the position that all texts are socially constructed. As texts are socially constructed, it follows that texts can be deconstructed and reconstructed for the purpose of changing problematic ways of being or doing.
- Text design and production can provide opportunities for critique and transformation (Janks, 1993; Larson & Marsh, 2005; Vasquez, 2005). This refers to the notion that before we are able to redesign a text, we must first figure out what about that text is so problematic that we need for it to be reconstructed. This process of figuring out what is problematic then creates a space for critique and transformation.

Inquiries Into Critical Literacy

It is hard to believe that 20 years have passed since I first began researching what it means to create spaces for critical literacy in the early-years classroom. It was between 1993 and 1996 that I, as a member of a teacher-research group, carried out two interrelated inquiries into critical literacy in practice. I worked first with children between the ages of 6 and 8 in a Grade 1/2 classroom and later with 3-to 5-year-olds (see Vasquez, 1994, 2000a, 2000b, 2000c). Both groups were representative of the very diverse, multiethnic, middle-class community in suburban Toronto in which the school was situated. With the aim of understanding how to construct a critical literacy curriculum, I produced observational narratives and gathered artifacts such as children's drawings and writing that I felt dealt with social justice and equity issues around the political and social topics talked about by my students and the questions they asked about these topics. While analyzing these artifacts of learning, I found that issues raised by the children led to conversations that moved well beyond the traditional topics of study often associated with primary school curriculum or mandated curriculum. For example, my students asked questions like, why are there no females in the advertisement poster of the Royal Canadian Mounted Police? Or, why do we have to have French class when no one in our class is French but we have lots of kids that speak Chinese? And, why can't we learn Chinese so we can talk to our friends? These questions became the focal elements in negotiating a critical literacy curriculum with my students. As a result, our curriculum consisted of rich experiences and deep understandings of social justice and equity issues. However, I was concerned that I had not always been able to generate further inquiry into social issues or make connections between such issues. I concluded that I had not gone far enough with critical literacy. Although I felt that my students and I engaged in powerful literacy work, I also felt that I had dealt with each critical literacy incident as isolated instances of learning. From reviewing the literature on critical literacy and preschool children, it became clear to me that very little had been done with critical literacy, and what had been done also took the form of isolated incidents. It was this combination of concerns and discoveries that led me to do another teacher-researcher study from 1996 to 1997.

My third inquiry into critical literacy took place in a junior kindergarten classroom where I worked with sixteen 3- to 5-year-old children, again representative of the diverse multiethnic community in what was known to be a middle-class neighborhood. In our class, there were nine ethnicities represented. There were 6 boys and 10 girls. Four of the boys were third-generation Canadian; one of the boys was Hispanic and the other Filipino. Of the nine girls, two were third-generation Canadian, two were second-generation Canadian, one was English-West Indian, one was Italian Canadian, another was Maltese Canadian, one was Portuguese, one was Polish, and one was Chinese. Five of the children in the class were from single-child homes or were the oldest of their siblings. The other 11 children had one or two older siblings. Eight of the children were 3 years old when the school year began, and the other eight were 4 years old. By the end of the year, half of the class had turned 4 and the other half had turned 5. Our class was a half-day morning junior kindergarten, and our school day was 8:45–11:15 AM. The school is publicly funded and located in what is considered a middle-class neighborhood in a suburb of Toronto, Ontario, Canada. Most of the homes in the vicinity of the school are single-home dwellings. This description is deceiving because there are a number of dual-family homes or homes where extended family members live together. Also,

FIG. I.2.   Our Classroom Audit Trail.

at the time of this research, Ontario was experiencing severe job cutbacks, which affected many families in the school.

Building on my previous two studies, I focused on using the issues from the social lives of children to construct and sustain a critical literacy curriculum. This time, my inquiry stretched over the course of a school year. I started on the first day of school and finished producing and gathering data on the last day of school. This time, the data took the form of an audit trail: a public display of artifacts (Fig. I.2).

An Amusement Park for Birds: The Influence of Reggio Emilia Documentation

During the summer preceding the school year, a colleague shared a video called *An Amusement Park for Birds* (Forman & Gandini, 1997). The video is a behind-the-scenes look at a long-term project at a Reggio Emilia school in Italy where young children researched, designed, and built an outdoor amusement park for birds in their school yard. The video included a segment on using documentation, which I found to be inspiring. I decided to read more (Cadwell, 1997; Hendrick, 1997) to further explore the way the teachers represented the children's learning through photographs, brief descriptions, and videos. Forman and Gandini (1997) define documentation as collecting information and artifacts produced by students for future reflection as a way to make visible the learning process of the children. They note that through this activity, the teacher discovers his or her own learning process as well. Documentation allows the steps and traces of learning of children and their teachers to be shared with other teachers and parents.

I liked the idea of making learning public and accessible to others, and I wondered what form such a public display might take. I was especially intrigued given the lack of narratives regarding critical literacy in practice available for teachers. I wondered what kind of impact a public display or documentation of our critical literacy work might have for my students and for myself, as well as the effect of such a display on parents and other colleagues. In Chapter 2, I detail how we got started with creating an audit trail as my take on documenting the learning process. I also talk about what we did to choose artifacts to document learning and how the audit trail became a site for negotiating a critical literacy curriculum and a site for assessing the children's learning. Before this however, in

Chapter 1, I begin by describing the context in which I negotiated a critical literacy curriculum with my students. I talk about how I negotiated such spaces within the mandated curriculum, along with the complexities involved with engaging in critical literacy practice. I also talk about various elements that were part of our school day and the role played by parents. I use the term *parent* to refer to a child's primary caregiver. In Chapters 3 through 6, I reconstruct a series of critical incidents represented on our audit trail as a way of making visible our critical work over the course of the school year. Aside from the reasons previously listed, I chose particular incidents I felt were thought provoking, interesting, and most clearly made visible the negotiation of a critical literacy curriculum using the children's questions about inequity. In a sense, these chapters tell a story that I hope will build a case for negotiating critical literacies with young children. At the end of these chapters, I have included Critical Reflections and Pedagogical Questions where I reflect briefly on the topics/issues raised and offer suggestions for consideration along with potential pedagogical moves. In the last chapter, I share some final thoughts regarding negotiating a year-long critical literacy curriculum with young children and discuss a special culminating experience that my students and I shared to bring closure to our year together.

1

Creating Spaces for Critical Literacy

Getting Beyond Prescriptive Curricula, the Mandated Curricula, and Core Standards

Although my students and I negotiated a critical literacy curriculum, which is described in detail in Chapter 2, we were not free from curricular mandates and the threat of standardized testing. Our school board dictated specific programs to follow (Fig. 1.1). As the classroom teacher, I made sure that I understood what was expected of me through the mandated curriculum in order to more readily map the work we were doing, our lived curriculum, against what was expected of us. Doing this made it much easier for me to articulate to parents, colleagues, and administrators the ways in which our negotiated curriculum surpassed the required curriculum (Fig. 1.2). I did this as a way of creating as much space as I could to engage in the literacy work that I felt would offer my students more opportunities for participating in the world by contributing to social change and that would give them access to more powerful literacies—that is, literacies that could make a difference in their

Personal And Social Studies

Meaningful Participation: The Individual in Society
• Identify some of their interests and values and some important relationships in their lives.
• Identify and describe their preferred learning activities.
• Contribute to school activities connected with an issue of concern.
• Demonstrate respect for the rights of others.
• Describe changes experienced.

Understanding Diversity and Valuing Equity
• Describe ways in which celebrations are observed by various cultures.
• Describe ways in which people make use of the world.

Understanding Natural and Human-Made Systems
• Describe personal experience of nature that inspires wonder.
• Identify local institutions and the work they do.
• Identify patterns that affect daily life.
• Participate in activities that help protect the environment.

Functioning in the Age of Information
• Talk about their work in their own words.
• Use a variety of forms to communicate ideas.
• Identify ways in which business gets consumers to notice their products.

Language

Listening and Speaking
• Retell stories told and/or read aloud.
• Use gestures, tone of voice and oral language structures to communicate.

Reading
• Use a variety of materials for information and pleasure.
• Use different strategies to respond to text.

Writing
• Write simple messages (e.g., labels, lists).
• Demonstrate some awareness of audience.

Viewing and Representing
• Use a variety of media text for entertainment and information.
• Explore stereotypes in the media.

Language for Learning
• Share ideas, experiences and information.
• Identify some forms of expression that are unfamiliar to particular individuals or cultures.

FIG. 1.1.   Sample Mandated Curriculum.

Mandated Curriculum	Our Negotiated Curriculum
Reading	
• Use a variety of materials for information and pleasure	• We used a variety of materials including picture books, magazines, resource books, Web sites, various cultural texts, art pieces, and music for information and pleasure.
• Use different strategies to respond to text	• We made use of code breaking practices, text analysis, various meaning making strategies, pragmatic practices, multiple sign systems, conversations, dramatizations, music, story telling, creating posters, journal writing, writing songs and poems, creating petitions, constructing surveys and many other strategies throughout the year.
Writing	Throughout the year we did the following kinds of writing:
• Write simple messages (e.g., labels, lists)	• letter writing • creating surveys • writing newsletters • composing songs • writing stories and poems • book writing • pamphlets and instruction sheets • warnings • reflections • day plans and meeting agendas
• Demonstrate some awareness of audience	• We sent surveys to other schools and petition letters to other classes in our school and our administrators. • We created posters for wood shops. • We wrote letters and newsletters to parents/guardians. • We sent letters to children in other countries. • We submitted a proposal to McDonald's.

FIG. 1.2.   A Chart Representing One Part of the Mandated Curriculum and a Sampling of What Was Covered Through Our Negotiated Curriculum.

lives, allowing them to participate differently in the world, for example, as young people, females, or underrepresented minorities.

Critical literacy, however, is not new, and there are growing accounts of teachers engaging in this practice. For example, Jenny O'Brien (1994) developed a unit of study around Mother's Day cards and flyers that she framed from a critical literacy perspective. Some of the things she had her students do included drawing and labeling six presents for mothers you expect to see in Mother's Day catalogs, drawing and labeling some presents you wouldn't expect to see in Mother's Day catalogs, or discussing what groups of people get the most out of Mother's Day. O'Brien's work offered the children an opportunity to consider a gendered cultural event, that is, an event that portrays mothers as being a certain way. The children then explored how these portrayals are connected to marketing and advertising, that is, how these portrayals lead to the selling of certain products associated with Mother's Day. This is the kind of activity that would give children tools to participate differently as consumers.

Another example is Maras and Brummett's (1995) study of the presidential elections. In Maras' classroom one year, they initiated what they thought would be a generative unit of study on life cycles. However, it was a presidential election year, and so the presidential elections lay foremost in the children's minds. As a result, the class engaged in a conversation through which a vote was organized regarding whether to return to the life-cycle agenda or to take on the presidential elections as an inquiry project. The vote was apparently one short of unanimous in favor of dropping the life-cycle study. As part of their inquiry into the elections, the children engaged in research both at home and at school. After dividing themselves into three campaign committees, for each of the presidential candidates—George Bush, Bill Clinton, and Ross Perot—the children read and discussed the newspaper and the news with their families at home. In school, they also discussed magazine articles and newspaper articles regarding the elections. This inquiry became the springboard for Maras and Brummett to build a unit of study framed from a critical literacy perspective. This newfound curriculum was no longer based on predetermined, prepackaged units of study but on the things that mattered to the children. Maras and Brummett contributed to writings on critical literacy by offering an example of how to draw from the issues central to the children's lives. They wrote about their experience with the presidential election project in Cordeiro's (1995) *Endless Possibilities*.

Critical Literacy as Pleasurable Work

My experience in working with teachers who attempt to engage in critical literacy shows me that, in many cases, social issues are treated as variables to be added to the existing curriculum. This is done rather than using the issues to build curriculum because these issues are associated with cynicism and unpleasurable work. However, critical literacy does not necessarily involve taking a negative stance; rather, it means looking at an issue or topic in different ways, analyzing it, asking questions such as those shared in the introduction chapter, and hopefully being able to suggest possibilities for change or improvement. Often issues of social justice and equity seem to be looked upon as heavy-handed issues. The conversations that we had and the actions we took, although often serious, were very pleasurable. We enjoyed our work because the topics that we dealt with were socially significant to us. As you read on, I believe this will become more and more evident, especially when you meet the children, read what they have to say, and become familiar with some of the life work they accomplished.

In my experience, the extent to which I was able to negotiate spaces to engage in critical literacy practices was related to the extent to which I had understood possibilities for engaging in critical literacies. The understanding or conceptualization that I am referring to is not about beliefs held in my head. The conceptualization I am referring to has to do with the extent to which I was able to act on my beliefs—in essence, to "do critical literacy theory." As my conceptualization of critical literacies changed, I was able to create different spaces for it in the curriculum, which led to further opportunities to deepen my understanding. These opportunities, in turn, led to the creation of even more curricular spaces. The relationship between conceptualization and negotiating spaces is therefore a recursive process (Fig. 1.3).

Deepening my conceptual understanding happened in a number of ways—engaging with critical literacy texts, hearing about others' attempts to engage in critical literacy practice, and working on critical literacy practices in my classroom or other local sites. Although this is true for me, your experiences may look very different. What I intend to do here is simply to give you an overview of the process through which my conceptualization of critical literacy developed. As reader, you will need to find strategies and supports that work best for you.

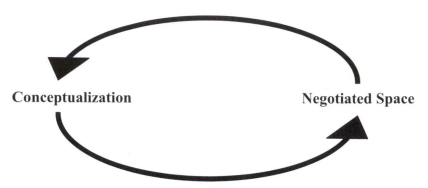

The better we are able to conceptualize critical literacies and act on our beliefs, the better able we are to create spaces for critical literacies. Subsequently, as we create more and more spaces we are better able to sort out how to better conceptualize critical literacies and create even more spaces for this work.

FIG. 1.3.   The Recursive Process of Conceptualization and Negotiating Curricular Spaces.

What Complexities Are Involved with Engaging in Critical Literacy Practice?

There are several questions that come to mind as I think about the complexities involved with engaging in critical literacies. Following are some of these questions:

What Does It Mean to Become Critically Literate?

For me, becoming critically literate had to do with framing my teaching from a critical literacy perspective and practicing critical literacies in my life outside of school. This does not mean that contestation and controversy have driven my life. In fact, having engaged in critical literacies has added a different layer of pleasure and productiveness to my life that is invigorating. I have had to come to an understanding of how I am both privileged and disadvantaged within different contexts and, in so doing, have found ways to actively participate in questioning inequities and injustices that arise in my life outside of as well as inside of school.

How Do I Go About Negotiating Spaces to Engage in Critical Literacies?

Comber and Cormack (1997) stated that literacy is constructed differently in different classrooms and across different contexts and school sites. Agreeing with this claim, I would suggest that the *where* of negotiating space and the *how* of negotiating space might differ also. The chapters that follow show that critical literacies can be negotiated "as curriculum" or "into the existing curriculum." The *as* and the *into* are important here. For me, they delineate engaging in a sustained and generative critical literacy curriculum or a curriculum based on isolated critical incidents.

My students and I created a yearlong integrated critical literacy curriculum for social justice and equity. We did not treat the issues raised as an add-on to the curriculum; that is, we did not add critical literacy as an extracurricular item. Nor did we treat social issues as unofficial classroom agenda. Instead, the issues became central to our curriculum; they became the stuff that our curriculum was made of.

Where Do I Find People to Support the Work I Am Doing?

As classroom teachers, we make sure our students' everyday lives include plenty of opportunities to learn from their peers. But often we do not worry about this for ourselves. As such, it is easy for us to become isolated in our classrooms. In my attempts at negotiating critical literacies in my classroom, I have sought out support both within my school community and in the larger professional community.

Support within the School Community

In some instances, engaging in critical literacies is seen as a subversive act that happens behind closed doors. In my school, people who were not directly involved in our day-to-day curriculum were more supportive because they were able to watch our curriculum take shape and to see the learning that took place through viewing our audit trail and through reading our class newsletters. They could see the connections we were making to both the official paper curriculum (e.g., skills associated with reading and writing) and what is often thought of as unofficial curricular topics (e.g., gender, the corporate agenda, marginalization).

Constructing an audit trail made our curriculum accessible for public conversation. Now and again interested colleagues and visitors to our school stopped by and asked us questions about the various artifacts on our wall. The visibility of our curriculum invited participation and created space for others to enter into our class discourse. The audit trail became a visual articulation of how my students and I negotiated an integrated critical literacy curriculum while dealing specifically with issues of social justice and equity that stemmed from my students' everyday lives. In Chapter 2, I have included the audit trail in its entirety.

Out-of-School Support Groups

Due to the fact that critical literacy is just recently taking root in early childhood classrooms, those of us who are attempting to engage in critical literacies have found it necessary to connect with others of like mind with whom to think through and share experiences. I would highly recommend either forming a study group or joining an existing one. You could start by contacting literacy organizations where you live or by contacting professional organization such as the Early Childhood Education Assembly of The National Council of Teachers of English (www.earlychildhoodeducationassembly.com) or the International Reading Association (www.reading.org). There are also courses now being offered at a number of universities.

Ending Teacher Isolation with Technology

Another opportunity to find others interested in critical literacy would be through joining listservs such as the one hosted by Rethinking Schools (www.rethinkingschools.org/archive/17_01/List171.shtml). Archives of the listserv are also available on their site. Or, if you participate in social networking, there are various groups that hold Twitter chats that are quite insightful and engaging. Signing up for this social networking tool is free and available at www.twitter.com. Twitter limits the sharing of information and discussion to 140 characters or less at a time. You can participate as little or as much as you are able. Placing a hashtag (#) in front of a word or phrase (no spaces) signifies a topic. For instance, #critlitchat signifies Twitter exchanges focused on critical literacy. Hashtags also help Twitter users to facilitate live conversations at certain times. For example, with the publication of this book, I will use the #critlitchat to engage in Twitter exchanges regarding the book. You can find out more about these chats at criticallite-racychat.blogspot.ca/. Educators from around the world who are interested in critical literacy can go online to talk about critical literacy by tagging their tweets with #critlitchat. Resource Box 1.1 lists a number of ways in which you can connect with me online.

Resource Box 1.1   Social Networking

Websites
www.vivianvasquez.com

Facebook
https://www.facebook.com/vivian.m.vasquez

Twitter
https://twitter.com/clippodcast

Pinterest
http://pinterest.com/criticallit/boards/

Pinterest

In the past, when a teacher had an idea to share, others might only find out about it by visiting his or her classroom or hearing about it in the teachers' lounge. Now Pinterest makes it easier to 'visit' other teachers' classrooms.

Organized visually, like a set of bulletin boards, Pinterest allows users to 'pin' photos of ideas they find on the Web. Pinterest also encourages users to follow one another (much like on Twitter) to see each other's pins and learn from others' discoveries.

Critical Literacy Chat
http://criticalliteracychat.blogspot.ca/

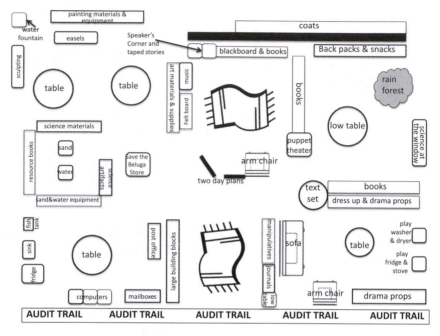

FIG. 1.4.   How Our Classroom Was Organized.

How Our Classroom Was Organized

I organized the classroom into different areas such as a class library and an area filled with art supplies (Fig. 1.4). Basically, I wanted to create an environment that would offer my students as varied a selection of resources and materials as possible. I also wanted these resources and materials accessible to them at all times. I did not want them to have to wait around for me to bring them the tools they needed for the work they were doing. Organizing the classroom into different areas made this possible. The children were quick to learn where things were stored and where things needed to be returned. This allowed me to spend more time discussing, researching, and playing with children. I also wanted to provide different kinds of workspaces and areas where my students could comfortably work on their own, in small groups and also as a large group.

How Our School Day Was Organized

For me, the school day started as the children arrived at the schoolyard. Issues and topics that were taken up in class often began as informal conversation in the yard. Each morning as the children entered the classroom, they signed in for attendance. After signing in, they looked over our job list to remind them of their responsibilities for the day. This was often done in pairs or small groups because some children were more familiar with decoding print than others. Early in the year, we created various jobs such as class botanist (the person in charge of looking after our plants), or class veterinarian (the person in charge of looking after our fish), as we needed them. While creating jobs in our classroom, we read about and discussed what a particular job entailed. Jobs were reassigned on a biweekly basis depending on who was interested in the various positions. Children who were leaving their jobs would train other children to take over. The children also checked to see if they were responsible for chairing our class meeting or for assisting the meeting chair. Once having signed in and having checked the job list, everyone except the person with the responsibility of chairing the class meeting spent time with books or worked on writing or drawing. At this time, the meeting chair circulated among the children asking if anyone had any items to add to the class meeting agenda, after which we began our class meeting. The children would add their agenda items by writing or drawing them on the class day plan, which consisted of chart paper posted on an easel board.

After our class meeting, the children chose different areas of the classroom to work on invitations or activities I had either created or negotiated with them, or they would work on their own topics (e.g., what it means to be a vegetarian), or issues (e.g., ways of collecting clothes for the flood victims in Manitoba). Invitations (Burke, 1998) are curricular experiences and engagements that provide learners opportunities to explore a topic, issue, or construct. For example, after analyzing a Halloween flyer based on how males and females are represented by the language used in describing costumes (e.g., mighty superhero vs. graceful ballerina), I created an invitation whereby students looked through a number of different advertisement flyers in order to think about how these public texts construct their understanding of the world. These invitations varied in number throughout the year. They represented one of the learning opportunities available to the children.

As the children explored their own questions, they worked independently or in small groups on research and then shared their thinking with others in the form of projects and presentations. Children would share with me the topics they were pursuing so that I could gather resources to support them. Other times they would go to the school library, which, lucky for us, was two doors away. Many

children also brought resources from home, particularly information gathered from the Internet. As the children engaged in various
learning experiences, I circulated among them and supported them
in various ways from listening to their ideas to offering suggestions
and resources as well as being their audience when they needed to
try out a presentation.

I think it is important to note that children were not rigidly
sitting at their desks working on invitations or their inquiries. Activities were spread out in different areas of the classroom. As children
engaged in their questions, they did so using different sign systems
(e.g., art, music, writing, math) and knowledge systems (e.g., science, social studies). They also moved about the room using various
materials and resources, as needed and where needed.

Previously, I gave you an idea of how the classroom and school
day were organized and talked a little about components of our
classroom day. In the next section, I talk briefly about a few other
common elements of our school day that had the biggest impact on
negotiating a critical literacy curriculum and the role of parents
within that curriculum.

Common Elements of Our School Day

Class Meeting

Class meetings were whole-group gatherings whereby individuals and small groups of children presented and discussed particular issues and topics with the whole class. These meetings began as
informal conversations. In fact, children could call an emergency
class meeting if they had a burning issue that they felt we needed to
address.

My intent was to be a participant in the meeting as opposed
to being the person in charge or the chair of the meeting, without implying that I was an innocent or neutral participant. One
of the concerns I had regarding child-centered pedagogies is the
attitude embedded in commonly heard statements such as "I had
nothing to do with it" (curriculum), or "It was all their idea," as
though the teacher's ideologies or beliefs never played a part in
what came to be curriculum. The bottom line is that children participate based on the discourses, the ways of being, that have been
made available for them, many of these having been introduced
at school.

The position of chairperson was offered to those children who wanted the job. As a group, we talked about what the chairperson's responsibilities would include, and then, those who were interested in the position were slotted on a calendar. A majority of the children volunteered to take a turn as chair. The role of chair became one of the major components of our class meetings as it gave the children a different status, allowing them more space to make decisions about how meetings might play out. Generally, a student would take on the role of chair or cochair (depending on their comfort level) for one week. At the completion of their turn as chair, part of their responsibility was to show the incoming chair the ropes, giving them advice and pointers if needed.

Setting a Meeting Agenda

Each class meeting was based on a meeting agenda that was developed at the start of every morning by the meeting chairperson. The agenda was created after signing in for attendance and checking to see what their job responsibilities were for the day. The individual whose job it was to be chair for the meeting moved about the room asking for items to be included in the meeting agenda. Items were topics, issues, questions, discoveries, and inquiries that children had. These items were then listed on poster board and propped up on a chart stand. Sometimes the children dictated their agenda items. Other times, the children took on this job for themselves, either writing using conventional or approximated spelling or drawing. Once all agenda items had been recorded in some way, the meeting began. Mostly this happened during the first 15 minutes of class. Often, children met me in the schoolyard sharing the issues they were interested in raising during class meeting. Even some of the parents showed interest and spoke with me of having had conversations with their children, while getting ready for school, regarding the issues/topics that their children were thinking about proposing for the meeting agenda.

Our meeting agenda became our shared day plan, our plan for working through the day. An example of these day plans can be found in Figure 1.5. In Figure 1.6, I outline the different components of the day plan. Because of the format we used, I had to keep a detailed account of the day in a separate binder. I did this for the purpose of substitute teachers in case I had to be away. Simply, this was made up of loose-leaf sheets of paper. These notes were done in narrative form and were written in a way that I hoped would be

Tuesday, May 27, 1997
Chair-Melissa

8:45   • Sign in for attendance
              • Check Jobs
              • Time with Books/Journals

Class Meeting Agenda Items	Reflections
1. May 26 Reflections →	Melissa and some other kids are going to write a letter today asking people for used clothes to send to the flood victims.
2. Melanie – J.K. Conference	
3. Gregory, Anthony & Stefanie – letter to families	
4. P.J. – Playing Fair	
5. Lily – Skirts →	In some countries boys wear dresses and skirts too.
	In the olden days boys and men wore night dresses for sleeping.
6. Ali & Lee - Power Rangers Change Again →	The show changed again. They do this so kids don't get bored. They change the shows so kids will keep watching.
	That's like McDonald's Happy Meals.
7. Michael – Cookie Day	
8. Alyssa – Art Techniques →	Showing something moving fast.
	See Andrew if you want to learn how to make things in your drawing look like they're moving.

10:10   Work Areas / Snack
              Play Practice
              Math Club

11:00   Campfire Songs
              Story – Nine O'clock Lullaby

11:15   Home

FIG. 1.5.   An Example of Our Day Plan.

Chair Person	Refers to the student who is in charge of running the class meeting.
Sign In	Children signed in for attendance.
Check Jobs	Different class members took on various responsibilities in the classroom.
Class Meeting Agenda	A time to negotiate our curriculum and raise issues of social justice and equity.
Reflections	A place to jot down thoughts, comments, questions and connections.
Work Areas	Different areas in the classroom to store and organize materials, resources and equipment.
Campfire Songs	Sharing songs and stories based on our current areas of interest.

FIG. 1.6.   Components of the Day Plan.

useful for substitute teachers and that would give them a sense of how we functioned as a classroom community.

Using Two Day Plans

As the year progressed, we began using two chart stands, one holding the current day's meeting agenda and day plan and the other holding the meeting agenda and day plan from the previous day. Both of these were put in a place where they were visible to the children gathered during meeting time (Figure 1.7). The decision to do this was made when I noticed the children often talked about items from previous discussions. On several occasions, they tried to turn the pages of the poster board to have a look at previous day plans while also referring to our current day plan. In conjunction with continually revisiting previous day plans, the children often got up from our meeting space and walked over to our audit trail, pointing at various artifacts that had been posted as a way of referring to past events and incidents and as a way of showing connections between events. I found this to be a very exciting example of how the children were connecting the different projects and other work we did over the course of the year. If you recall from the introduction, I talked about doing the third inquiry due to frustration that in the past I felt unsuccessful at connecting the various critical literacy

FIG. 1.7.   Using Two Day Plans.

incidents. The use of the learning wall and the two shared day plans obviously helped to alleviate that concern.

Reflections

A reflection section was added to our daily agenda after one of the children asked me, "What are those things you are writing on the side of the agenda?" The child was referring to my jottings and notations along the margins of our day plan. I responded by saying that I was jotting down thoughts, my reflections, regarding things we were discussing as we talked about each agenda item. Subsequently, in conversation with the class about the use of reflections, the children asked me if we could always have reflections along the side of our day plan so that they could do some reflecting also.

I created a reflection section (Fig. 1.8) by drawing a line down the right side of the poster board. It was added as a place to jot down thoughts about issues raised and connections made to previous conversations. The reflections eventually became the first items discussed at all meetings. Using reflections was a way for us to revisit what we had discussed during the preceding meeting and to

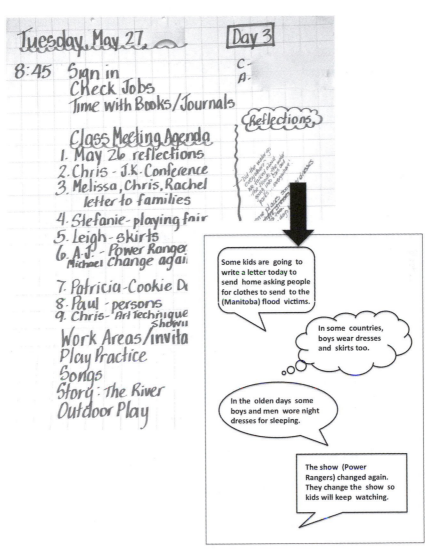

FIG. 1.8. Reflections.

connect our current learning with our learning from the past. This became yet another way for us to make connections between the various issues. Comments or questions were then raised regarding the reflections. Now and again, the children would refer to these reflections in order to make decisions about what items to put on future meeting agendas.

Read-Aloud

Read-aloud was a time when I shared books with the children or when children shared books with one another based on what we were currently studying. It took place at different times, before, during, or after class meetings. Time was flexible depending on what books we were sharing and for what reasons. For example, I would start the day with a read-aloud if I had a book I wanted to share based on an issue or topic that came up the previous day. Most often the books chosen for read-aloud were part of a text set of children's literature (combination of books and everyday texts that are based on the same topic or that offer different perspectives on the same topic) and everyday texts.

Whole-Group Wrap-Up

This gathering took place at the end of each day. It was a brief whole-group gathering to reflect on what we had done throughout the day and to consider possibilities for the following school day. This was also a time to share connections and questions as well as a time to share songs, poetry, or stories. Sometimes seeds for meeting agenda items were planted during this time.

The Role of Parents/Guardians

Eight out of the 16 children in the classroom were placed in my room as a result of requests made by parents. These parents were aware of the ways in which I had negotiated curriculum with children the previous year and my critical literacy take on negotiating curriculum with children. Some of them had older children who had been in my class in the past. They appreciated my belief that children are capable of more than what the traditional junior kindergarten or preschool curriculum offered. In a sense, I was in a position of privilege, having parents who supported my theoretical and pedagogical stance from the start. These relationships, however, did not happen instantly but rather developed over time through ongoing discussion and conversation about learning and literacy.

Prior to the first day of school, I held an open house and meeting with the parents/guardians to share my thinking about negotiating a critical literacy curriculum with the new parents and to renew connections with those with whom I had previously worked. I had phone conversations with those who were unable to attend or visited with them in their homes. These first meetings were my attempt to begin a dialogue about learning as well as to let the parents/guardians know how important maintaining ongoing communication would be for their children's learning, and in helping to inform the curricular decisions I would have to make.

This ongoing dialogue took different forms, depending on the family schedules and time restraints. Some parents/guardians touched base with me on a daily basis as they were dropping off or picking up their child. Others sent notes to school with their child; still others maintained written communication with me using a written conversation notebook. Other parents called to talk over the phone on a regular basis. It took a lot of extra time, effort, and coordination to keep lines of communication open, but I felt that the support I received as a result of these efforts far exceeded the energy I had expended. I also held three open dialogue nights at school where parents who were unable to visit during the day could come in to talk about issues, questions, and comments regarding their child's learning in an informal group setting. This was a social gathering time as well as a time to look at artifacts that had been posted on our audit trail. Being able to spend time together to talk about the artifacts on our audit trail was important to the work that the children and I did. I realized that the audit trail could be read in many different ways. The children and I read it from a critical literacy perspective because that was the history we had shared. I knew that if the parents were privy to that history, they too could impact the issues we were dealing with in the classroom and that this could hopefully create spaces for our classroom conversations to overflow into the home. I didn't want the colorfulness and aesthetic appeal of the audit trail to be seen as uncritical or dismissed as a "cute bulletin board idea."

Also prior to the first day of school, children and their families had a chance to visit our classroom, and/or I had a chance to visit with them in their homes. Those who were able to make the visit saw the empty bulletin board space and heard about my intention of negotiating a critical literacy curriculum with the children. Those who were not able to visit heard about my intentions through a class newsletter. These visits were opportunities for me to learn as much as I could about my students. Cristina Igoa (1995) emphasized the importance of home–school interaction, stating that it gave her the opportunity to assist the child in finding a connection between home and school. If I wanted the critical literacies learned by my students to have an impact beyond the walls of our classroom, I knew that maintaining lines of communication with the home would be crucial.

In the next chapter, I begin to tell the story of negotiating a critical literacy curriculum with my students by describing an incident that took place during our first read-aloud session.

2

Getting Started:
Setting the Scene

Constructing a Curricular Audit Trail

It was the first day of school with my sixteen 3- and 4-year-old students. I decided to start the day with a read-aloud of a picture book that I thought the children would find interesting and that had a patterned predictable text so they could read with me. The book I chose was Don and Audrey Wood's (1993) *Quick as a Cricket*. I read,

> I'm as quick as a cricket,
> I'm as slow as a snail,
> I'm as small as an ant,
> I'm as large as a whale.
>
> I'm as sad as a basset,
> I'm as happy as a lark,
> I'm as nice as a bunny,
> I'm as mean as a shark.
> I'm as cold as a . . .

"Is that a frog or a toad?" asked 4-year-old Gregory. (Please note that the names appearing throughout the book are pseudonyms.) He was referring to an illustration of an amphibian sitting on a rock (Fig. 2.1). "How can we find out?" I responded. I had a number of different resource books in the classroom on a broad range of topics. As we looked through the books, one of the things I suggested was to compare the environment in the *Quick as a Cricket* illustration to the environment that the frogs and toads lived in as depicted in a variety of books. Together we hypothesized that one way to tell whether the amphibian is a frog or toad is through its environment.

This initial exchange regarding whether or not the illustration in the book was that of a frog or toad generated a series of issues and topics such as rain forests, the environment, and gender. Capitalizing on these issues, I began to develop a curriculum based on our

FIG. 2.1.
Frog or Toad
Illustration.

class conversations and my observations of the children as noted in the introduction chapter (see Fig. I.1).

Choosing Artifacts

To represent our initial conversation regarding Gregory's question—"Is that a frog or toad?"—I decided to post the book cover (Fig. 2.2), a copy of the illustration (Fig. 2.1), and Gregory's question. The combination of artifacts initially posted on our empty bulletin board is shown in Fig. 2.3. Once I posted these first three artifacts, I talked to the children about why I felt each one best represented our conversation about frogs and toads and then asked them to think about different things we could use to remind us of incidents and questions that came up in our classroom. We

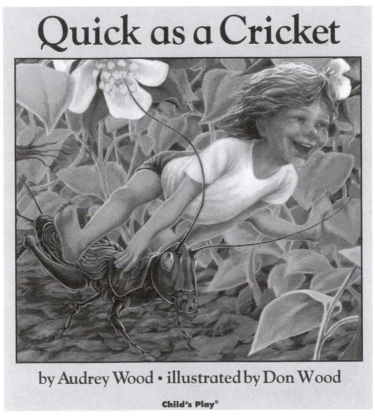

FIG. 2.2. *Quick as a Cricket* Book Cover.

FIG. 2.3. The First Artifacts Posted on Our Audit Trail.

brainstormed various possibilities, creating a list that included drawings, pictures, cutouts from magazines, book covers, and writing. Examples of artifacts that were posted on our bulletin board, that is, our audit trail, are included throughout the book.

What Is an Audit Trail?

An audit trail is a visual articulation of learning and thinking that is meant to be visible not only to the people in a classroom community but to others in the school community as well (Harste & Vasquez, 1998). This public visibility makes the audit trail a participatory site for becoming involved in the children's learning. Students and teachers research their world together and produce representations of that research, in the form of an audit trail, that is displayed on a bulletin board, or other surface, covered with various artifacts of learning. Throughout the year, previous learning events can be revisited using the artifacts as trigger images that serve as reminders of work done and the learning that has taken place.

Using an Audit Trail as a Tool for Generating, Constructing, and Circulating Meaning

Retracing thinking involves theorizing. As my students and I began constructing an audit trail, I thought about using it as a tool for critical conversation with them. It seemed to me that making theoretical connections visible using artifacts might enable my students to revisit, reread, analyze, and reimagine possibilities for living a critically literate life. I also imagined that the audit trail could be a tool for building curriculum. The children referred to the audit trail as The Learning Wall because they said the wall was all about their learning. Throughout this book, I use the terms audit trail and learning wall interchangeably. Artifacts included photographs, book covers, posters, newspaper clippings, magazine ads, transcripts of conversations, a stuffed toy, and Internet printouts representing our theories of the world about things that mattered to us. Each of the artifacts became a way for us to make visible the incidents that caused us to want to learn, the issues we had critical conversations about, and the actions we took to resist being dominated and to reposition ourselves within our community. The audit trail became our demonstration of and our site for building a critical curriculum for ourselves. Over the course of the school year, the children regularly referred to various artifacts on the audit trail, often pointing to the artifacts that were posted. Issues recorded on the audit trail generated curriculum topics including rainforests, the environment, gender, fairness, the media, and a range of questions concerned with power and control. Over a period of 10 months, various issues were sustained and continuously revisited on our learning wall that grew to be a 40-foot by 6-foot length of wall space consisting of over 130 artifacts. The audit trail we constructed throughout the year is included in its entirety as Figure 2.4 Section 1 to Section 38.

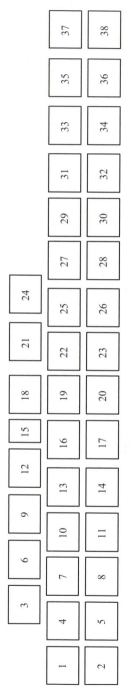

FIG. 2.4. Map and Sections of Our Audit Trail.

FIG 2.4. Section 1.

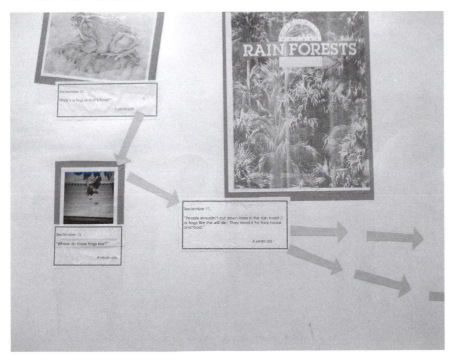

FIG. 2.4. Section 2.

FIG. 2.4.   Section 3.

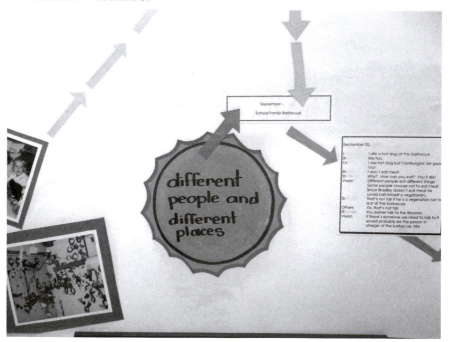

FIG. 2.4.   Section 4a.

September 20,

Leigh	I ate a hot dog at the barbecue.
Stefanie	Me too.
Omar	I ate hot dog but hamburgers are good too!
Bradley	I don't eat meat.
Stefanie	Why? How can you eat? You'll die!
Vivian	Different people eat different things. Some people choose not to eat meat. Since Bradley doesn't eat meat he could call himself a vegetarian...
Stefanie	That's not fair if he's a vegetation not to eat at the barbecue.
Others	Ya, that's not fair.
Stefanie	You better talk to the librarian.
Vivian	If there's someone we need to talk to it would probably be the person in charge of the barbecue,

FIG. 2.4.   Section 4b.

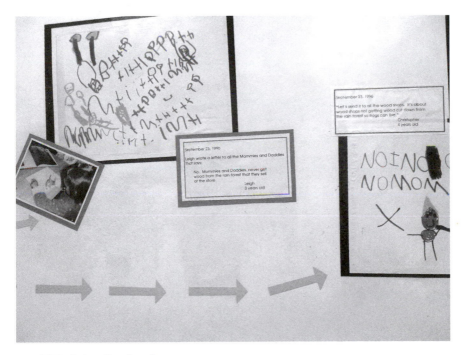

FIG. 2.4.   Section 5a.

September 23

"Let's send it to all the wood shops. It's about wood shops not getting wood cut down from the rain forest so frogs can live."

4 years old

FIG. 2.4. Section 5b.

FIG. 2.4. Section 6.

FIG. 2.4. Section 7.

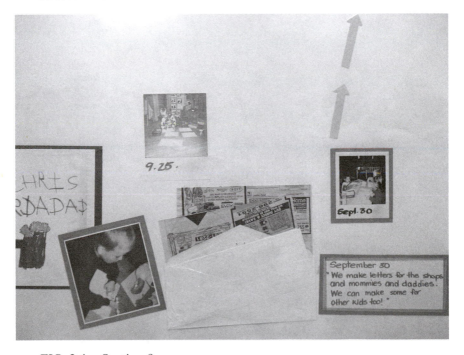

FIG. 2.4. Section 8.

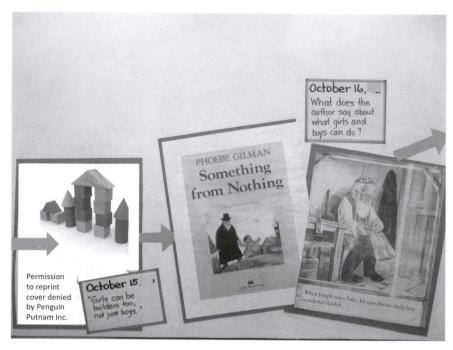

FIG. 2.4.   Section 9.

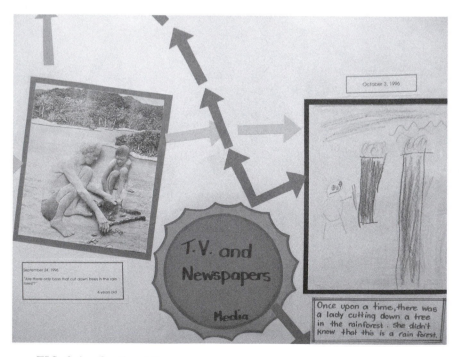

FIG. 2.4.   Section 10.

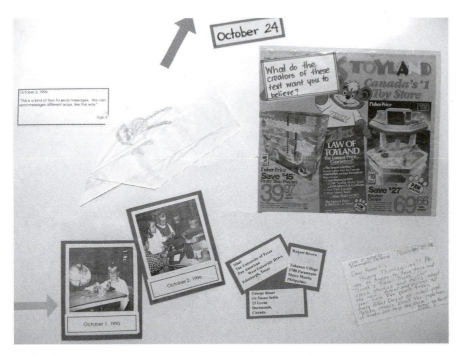

FIG. 2.4.   Section 11.

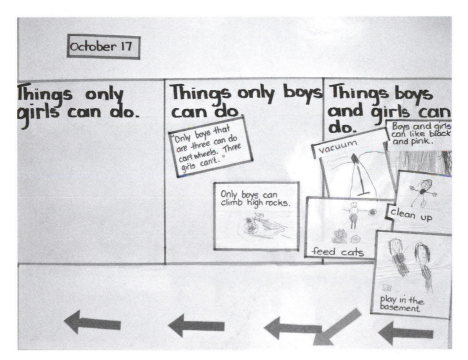

FIG. 2.4.   Section 12.

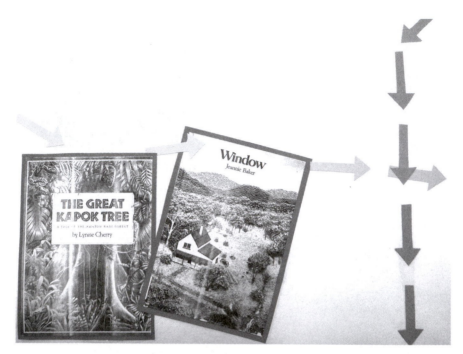

FIG. 2.4. Section 13.

FIG. 2.4. Section 14.

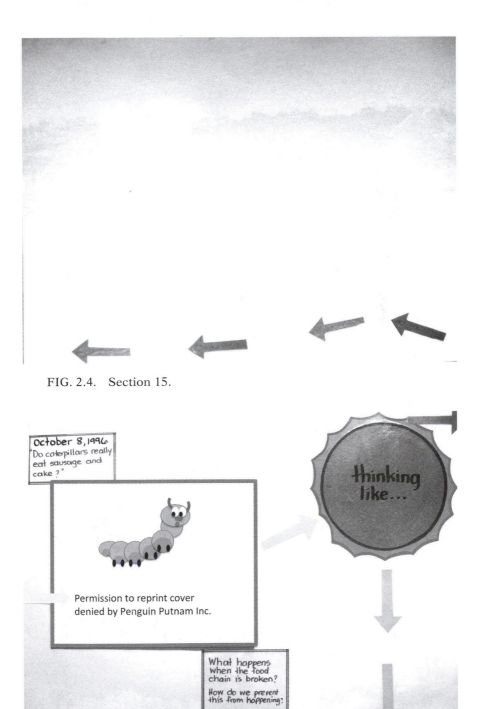

FIG. 2.4.   Section 15.

FIG. 2.4.   Section 16.

FIG. 2.4.   Section 17.

FIG. 2.4.   Section 18.

FIG. 2.4.   Section 19.

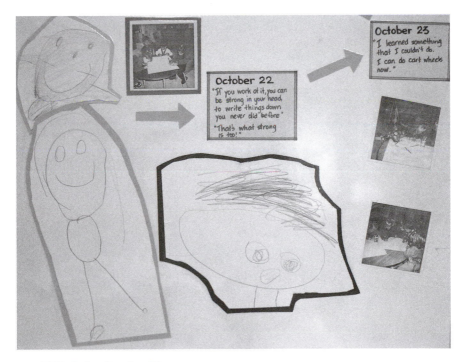

FIG. 2.4.   Section 20.

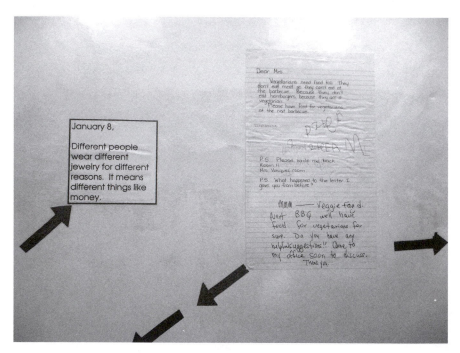

FIG. 2.4.　Section 21.

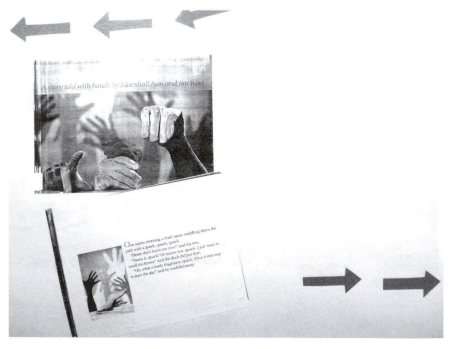

FIG. 2.4.　Section 22.

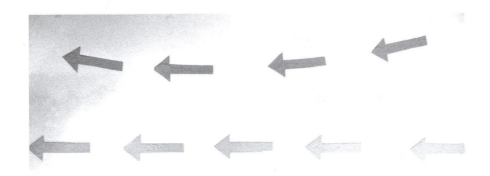

FIG. 2.4.   Section 23.

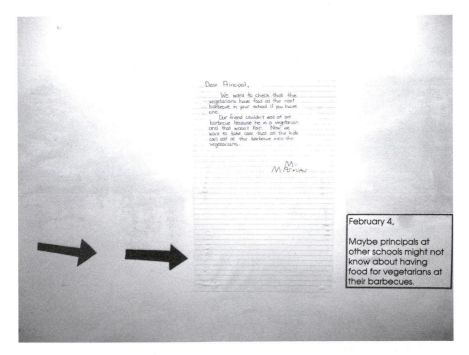

FIG. 2.4.   Section 24.

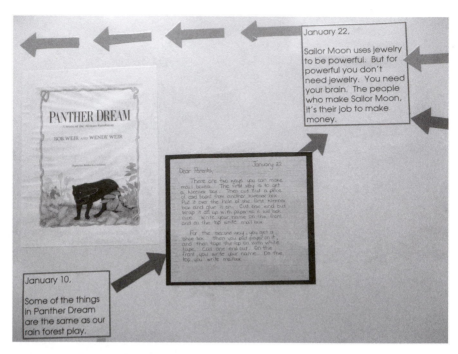

FIG. 2.4.　Section 25.

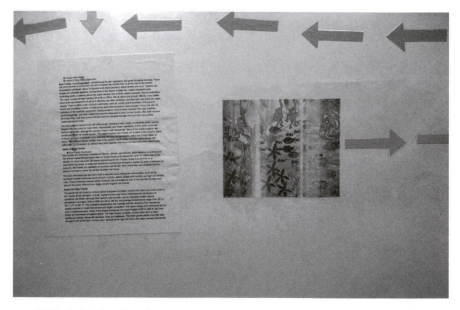

FIG. 2.4.　Section 26.

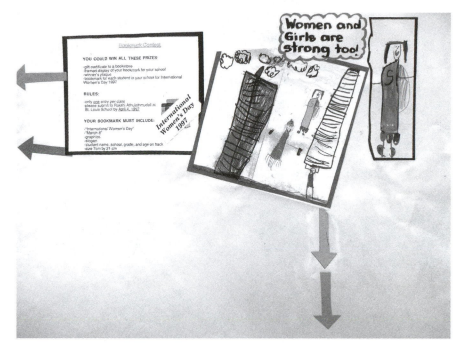

FIG. 2.4.   Section 27.

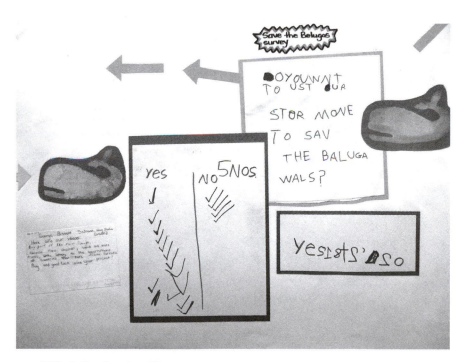

FIG. 2.4.   Section 28.

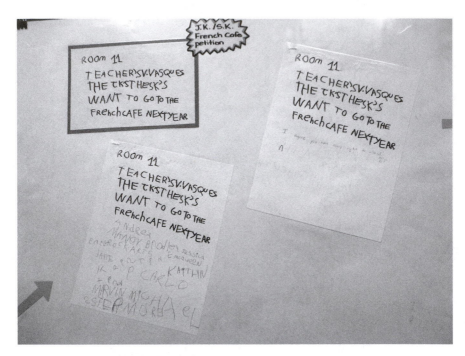

FIG. 2.4.   Section 29.

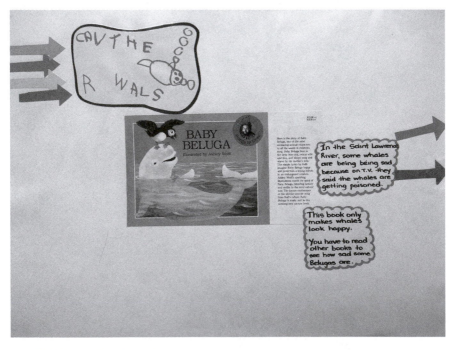

FIG. 2.4.   Section 30.

FIG. 2.4.   Section 31.

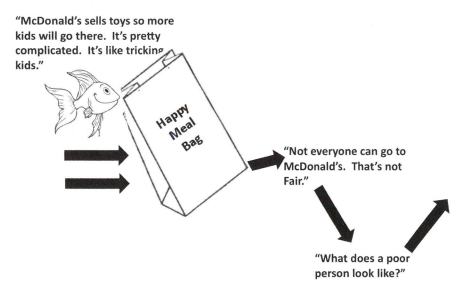

FIG. 2.4.   Section 32.

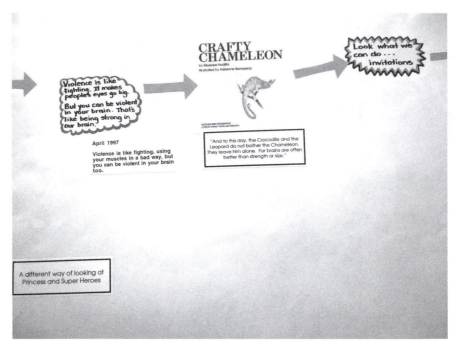

FIG. 2.4.　Section 33.

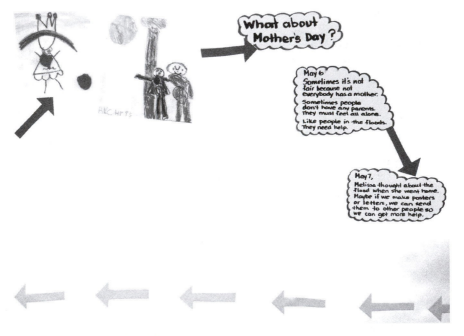

FIG. 2.4.　Section 34.

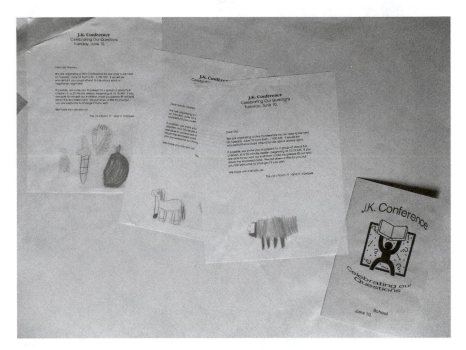

FIG. 2.4.   Section 35.

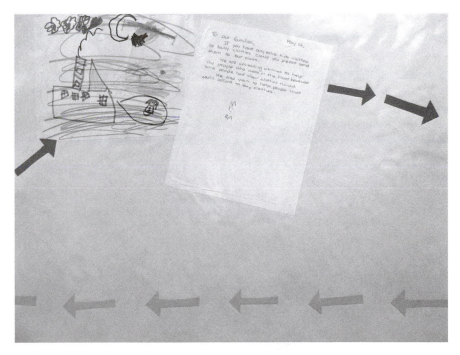

FIG. 2.4.   Section 36.

What next year's J.K.'s should know

Listen to the other kids

Remember other people's feelings

If there's something happening in the school and you want to go, you can make something like petitions.

Boys and girls should share their feelings and talk and not fight.

You have to share with the other kids

Put things away after you use them

You can be strong from your brain

You should know that McDonalds and the newspaper and books and schools can make you think their way.

FIG. 2.4.   Section 37.

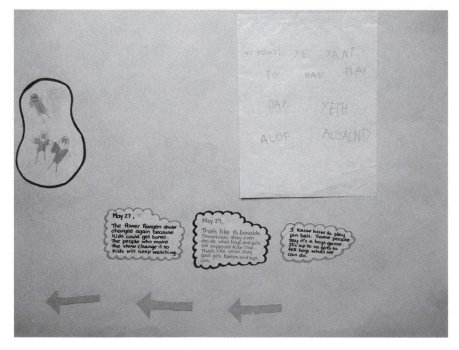

FIG. 2.4.   Section 38.

The Audit Trail Grows

Our initial question, "Is this a frog or a toad?" led to inquiry into amphibian environments. One of the environments that most interested the children was the rain forest. As a result, an inquiry into rain forests began. I created various engagements and curricular activities that included opportunities for my students to think about and analyze various books and everyday texts related to this topic. For example, as part of our study of rain forests, I asked the children to collect newspaper reports, magazine articles, songs, and other texts about rain forests. We then looked at these various items and talked about similar and different ways that particular environmental issues are reported or represented. While doing this, a group of children found a song in a children's book. They liked the song because they said it was about saving the animals that live in rain forests, which was an issue that had become important to them.

Creating a Rain Forest Play

After learning the song, some of the children began acting out parts of it. I suggested to them that acting out parts of the song was a good way of representing what we were learning about saving the rain forests and that drama was a good way of sharing with others what we had learned. Some of the children immediately wanted to sing and dramatize the song for the children in our school. I told them if this was their intent, they needed to develop the drama and rehearse it before performing it for others. The result was the creation of the rain forest play. A script was written for the play (Fig. 2.5) and a set (Fig. 2.6) in which to perform the play was created. The play was our way of helping other children in our school to learn about the need to preserve rain forests and to send a message regarding what happens when rain forests are harvested for profit. We talked about who benefits from such practices and the damage to the environment and animal habitats.

This particular social action was highlighted on our audit trail by posting the list of characters in the play (Fig. 2.7).

Developing the play from conceptualizing what the main message would be, scripting, planning costumes, creating the set, and then organizing a schedule to perform the play for various audiences (other classes, parents) took around 3 weeks and involved everyone in the class in varying capacities.

The Rainforest Play

Cast of Characters

    P Person cutting down rainforest trees
    S Saver of the rainforest
    F Frog
    Sn Snake
    B Butterfly

Dialogue

P   (Walks into the rainforest with an axe and starts cutting trees)

           I'm going to the rainforest to chop all the trees.

S   Stop!

P   Why?

S   Because we won't have any animals left in the rainforest!

P   Why?

S   Because we won't have air to breathe.

           Here comes my friend frog.

P   I don't see anybody.

F   Ribbit ribbit. If you chop down those trees I won't have

           any place to live or to eat.

Sn   If you do that I won't have a place to live.

B   Even me, I won't have a place to eat too!

S   See, there are animals here!

All   The End.

FIG. 2.5.   Script for the Play.

FIG. 2.6.   Rainforest Play Backdrop.

The following text appears within the figure:

L I can be the one who cuts down the trees.
C You can be a logger!
L Okay.
M I'll be the rainforest frog.
S What am I called?
M A caterpillar.
A I'm a beautiful butterfly.
L I'll say, I'm going to the rainforest now. I'll go like
   this to pretend I'm cutting down a tree.

FIG. 2.7.   Characters in the Play.

Other types of action that resulted from our initial inquiry included writing a letter to the parents in our class asking them not to buy wood that has been harvested from rain forests (Fig. 2.8). We also sent a poster to all "woodshops" (places that sell wood) asking them not to sell wood that has been harvested from rain forests (Fig. 2.9). The letter to the parents was included with an explanation in our class newsletter, and the letter to the woodshops was mailed to different lumberyards in the city where our school is located. Creating the poster and letter resulted from conversations regarding the economics involved in producing goods made using wood from rain forests, that is, conversations about buyers, sellers, and producers. For example, we talked about what the benefits were for people who sell, buy, or produce wood.

Raising Issues of Gender

Gender equity was another issue that arose from our study of rain forests. While reading *Where the Forest Meets the Sea* (Baker,

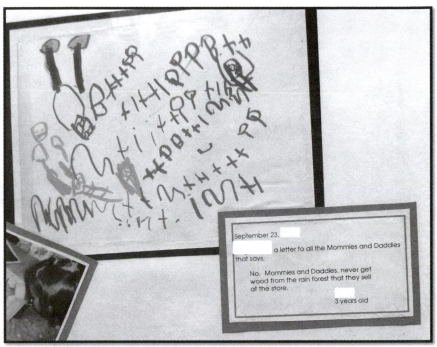

September 23, ▮▮▮

▮▮▮ a letter to all the Mommies and Daddies
that says:

No. Mommies and Daddies, never get
wood from the rain forest that they sell
at the store.

▮▮▮

3 years old

FIG. 2.8.   Letter to the Parents and Guardians.

FIG. 2.9. Letter to the Wood Shops.

1998), the issue of gender came up when one of the children asked, "Why is it a man and not a woman cooking?" regarding a particular illustration (Fig. 2.10). This marked the beginning of our study about gender equity. The question led to the analysis of various texts. I made use of O'Brien's (1994) interrogation of Mother's Day cards as a framework for considering ways to interrupt dominant ways of talking about gender in various texts, specifically everyday texts such as television commercials and magazine ads as well as picture books. We began to look at these texts asking questions like:

- What roles are given to males?
- What roles are given to females?
- Who are the powerful characters?
- Who are the weak characters?
- Do you know people in your life who are like the characters in the book?

FIG. 2.10. *Where the Forest Meets the Sea* Illustration.

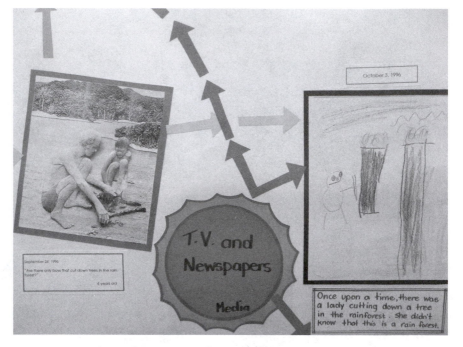

FIG. 2.11. Gender Issue Artifacts Posted on Our Audit Trail.

- What are things you know people can do that the characters in the book can't do?
- What can we do to change the story?
- Who is telling the story?
- Why might they be telling the story in that way?

These questions became discussion starters that helped me to develop other learning experiences.

To represent the incident regarding gender on our audit trail, the children patterned the artifacts they chose after those that I used to represent the "frog or toad" and "rain forest" issues. They chose a copy of the book cover, the illustration, and the question "Are there only boys that cut down trees in the rain forest?" (Fig. 2.11).

Gender was taken up several more times over the course of the year as we worked with various everyday texts such as newspaper flyers and magazine ads. Through our discussions, we explored how society constructs what males and females can and cannot do and ways in which this happens. For example, on our audit trail, we posted an ad flyer that was brought to class by one of the children. This particular flyer was used as a springboard to talk about how newspaper ads are constructed, the language used in the ads, why they are produced in the first place, how they represent life options, who creates and distributes these flyers, and how we, as consumers and buyers, use them to make particular decisions about who we want to be and how we want to be in the world. By doing this kind of work, we engaged in text analysis (Freebody & Luke, 1990). For example, one instance of text analysis involved problematizing or asking questions about Halloween costume ads as well as analyzing the ad contents. We asked questions such as the following:

- Who is represented wearing certain kinds of costumes?
  - What costumes were young boys wearing?
  - What costumes were young girls wearing?
  - What costumes were older boys wearing?
  - What costumes were older girls wearing?
- Which costumes cost more?
- Which cost less?
- Which costumes represent people with power? Who is wearing these?
- In what ways do these costumes tell you what you can and cannot be?

As a result of our discussion, some of the children designed their own costumes to counter those in the ad. We also looked at the language used to describe the costumes and how the describing words associate certain characteristics with boys and other characteristics with girls.

Audit Trail as a Tool for Constructing Curriculum

What you have read so far represents only the beginning of the work we did over the course of the school year, along with some of the ways that different inquiries were born and ways that inquiries were connected. Issues continued to be generated and connected throughout the year. Our audit trail became an important tool, an important technological site for constructing and negotiating curriculum, and for building a shared curricular history. Our curriculum was therefore participatory in that children were not just consumers of curriculum; rather, they helped to construct curriculum through their contributions to class discussion such as during meeting times. As various items were added to our audit trail, each became an artifact with a history that reflected the children's thinking and learning during different periods of time throughout the year.

Other issues that were generated and how they connect to one another can be found in Table 2.1. These figures outline the various questions and topics that we negotiated, the context in which the issue unfolded, the curricular engagements used, the actions taken, and other issues that were generated. A second table (Table 2.2) lists the various artifacts we posted. This table consists of 18 parts with each part divided into three columns. The first column contains the artifact, the second column describes the artifact, and the third column outlines the issue(s) represented by the artifact. Further, detailed descriptions of how issues or topics were generated are included at www.vivianvasquez.com.

TABLE 2.1

Chart Representing Issues on Our Audit Trail

Issue(s)	Context	Curricular Engagements	Actions	Other Issues Generated
1. Rainforests are in danger. What can we do to help save the rain forest?	While sharing the book *Quick as a Cricket* during the first few days of school, the children paused at one of the illustrations asking whether the animal shown is a frog or a toad. This initial question led to conversations about where frogs and toads live. One of the habitats we talked about was the rain forest.	• Letter writing. • Research into the rain forest. • Poster design. • Locating places to send travel trunks on the globe. • Organizing travel trunks. • Writing a script for a play about the rainforest. • Creating a schedule to perform the play for other classes.	• Letter to parents/ guardians asking them not to buy wood from shops that sell products harvested from rain forests. • Created a poster that was sent to lumber yards reminding them not to buy wood from companies who violate rain forests. • Created rain forest travel trunks to help inform children in other classrooms around the world regarding the violation of rain forests.	• Interconnectedness of life. • The need to help others. • The need for food and shelter. • Gender issues. • Perspectives: Thinking like an Artist Scientist Mathematician Geographer

(continued on next page)

TABLE 2.1 (*continued*)

Issue(s)	Context	Curricular Engagements	Actions	Other Issues Generated
1. (*continued*)		• Designing a backdrop for the play. • Creating invitations and information sheets for people coming to see the play that contains facts and resource lists on books and organizations that support saving the rain forests of the world.	• Wrote a play to teach other kindergartens in the school about rain forests.	

| 2. What has happened to the trees that were once in our neighbor-hoods? | As part of our rain forest conversations, children began to compare the trees they saw in books about the rain forest to those in our neighborhood. They wondered about why the trees in the school neighborhood are so small. They theorized that they must be newly planted trees which led them to wonder whether there once were older trees and if there were what happened to them.

 This resulted in a conversation about how land is cleared by builders to build houses. | • Researching what Mississauga used to look like before builders began buying off land.

 • Walking around the community to observe the kinds of trees that currently exist. | • Letters to a local builder. | • Animal Rights: What happens to the animals who live in areas where trees are cut down and the land is cleared? |

(continued on next page)

TABLE 2.1 (*continued*)

Issue(s)	Context	Curricular Engagements	Actions	Other Issues Generated
3. Gender and how society decides what males and females can and cannot do and who they could and should be.	While reading *Where the Forest Meets the Sea* as part of our inquiry into rain forests, the children began interrogating a particular illustration of a man cooking over an open fire. One of the children asked why it is a man cooking and not a woman. This question created space for a conversation on gender.	• Created a picture graph of things girls, boys, girls and boys can do. • Analyzing the graph. • Interrogating children's literature to look at how boys and girls are positioned and how males and females are positioned.	• Deliberate attempts were made by the children in the classroom not to let gender decide (e.g., who can play what games, who can play with what toys).	• How do newspaper flyers position girls and boys, males and females?

4. It is unfair for vegetarians at our school and other schools not to have food that they can eat.	The day after our school barbecue the children initiated a conversation regarding how the barbecue had gone, what people had eaten, and what people had done. As part of this conversation, one of the children shared that he was not able to eat at the barbecue because he is vegetarian. Linking this incident with the issue of needing food and shelter as generated through our rain forest inquiry led to problematizing the choices for food at the school barbecue.	• Research on vegetarians. • Letter writing. • Designing and mailing out a survey.	• Wrote two letters to the organizer of the school barbecue. • Sent a survey and note to other schools regarding the need to find out whether there are vegetarians at different sites who are not considered when making meal plans at different school functions and events.	• Difference and diversity. • How are some people marginalized at our school, in our community, and in other places?

(continued on next page)

TABLE 2.1 (*continued*)

Issue(s)	Context	Curricular Engagements	Actions	Other Issues Generated
5. Who is left out of the books we have in our library?	While researching about vegetarians (issue #4), a group of children discovered that we did not have any books on vegetarians in the school library. This led to a conversation regarding who else may not be represented by the books and resources in our school library.	• Memo writing. • Chart of things that represent us. [The chart created represents who we are, either through something that we are interested in or our cultural heritage.]	• Wrote a memo to the librarian regarding what books should be purchased for the library.	• Books as representing specific versions of the world.

6. Unequal Distribution of Power: How are kindergarten students positioned in our school, by the larger educational community?	One day a flyer was sent to our classroom regarding a contest for International Womens Day. The contest involved creating a bookmark for this day and including a slogan in support of women. The interest in womens rights and gender had been sustained from an earlier conversation described in issue #3 that took place earlier in the year. The children wanted to know more about the contest so I called the organizers to find out more about it.	• Designing and measuring [the book mark had to be a specific size]. • Creating slogans. • Researching other bookmarks to decide on what to include.	• Entered a bookmark contest.	• What other events, competitions, activities are there in which kindergarten students are not considered?

(continued on next page)

TABLE 2.1 *(continued)*

Issue(s)	Context	Curricular Engagements	Actions	Other Issues Generated
6. *(continued)*	I discovered and shared with the children that the contest is predominantly entered by older students. This started a discussion of the ways in which kindergarten students are marginalized in our school as well as in the broader educational community.			

7. What other things can we do to change things that are not equitable or things that are unfair in our school, in our community, in the world?	Involvement in the bookmark competition resulted in an awareness that not all age groups of children are treated equitably and that the kindergartens in particular, are often seen as not being capable of certain actions. As the school announcements were being made over the PA system, a group of children became aware of an event called the French Café which was being held at our school. One of them theorized from the announcement that everyone but the kindergarten students were being invited to the café.	• Survey research: Who is going to the café • Letter writing. • Creating a Speakers Corner tape. • Creating a petition and collecting signatures.	• Petition. • Speaker's Corner tape • Age Equity • Respect and Understanding

(continued on next page)

TABLE 2.1 (*continued*)

Issue(s)	Context	Curricular Engagements	Actions	Other Issues Generated
8. Save the Beluga and animal rights.	Since having engaged in inquiry regarding rain-forests, other environmental issues became of interest to the children. One day during class meeting one of the children reported a story she heard on the evening news regarding the plight of the Beluga whales in the St. Lawrence River. She learned that pollution was causing the whales to die off.	• Problematizing the text "Baby Beluga" and thinking about how it could be otherwise. • Recreating/rewriting stories that offer another perspective. • Rewrote the "Baby Beluga" Song by Raffi.	• Save the Beluga store: Money made was sent to World Wildlife Fund of Canada.	• Animal rights. • Endangered species. • Responsibility and citizenry.

| 9. McDonald's: The Corporate Agenda | As a result of the conversation regarding the beluga whales, the children started to talk about how powerless the whales are and how humans control their destiny. This led to further discussions regarding power and control, including how corporations and the media control the decisions we make as consumers. To contextualize the conversation, one of the children made the comment that "it is just like McDonald's." This then led to a discussion about the corporate agenda as a money-making institution that uses and manipulates consumers for their own profit. | • Researched and analyzed flyers and ads.

• Created a series of web maps to show how McDonald's, Burger King and other fast food companies work to actively seek out consumers, particularly children, to buy their food and various toy products.

• Letter writing. | • McDonald's boycott. | • What other actions can we take to expose and interrogate the corporate agenda?

• How do clothing manufacturers do the same thing that the fast food companies do?

• How do clothing manufacturers and places like McDonald's tell you what it means to be male and female? |

(continued on next page)

TABLE 2.1 (continued)

Issue(s)	Context	Curricular Engagements	Actions	Other Issues Generated
10. Manitoba flood victims	Previous conversations about gender issues and media control led us to talk about how mothers are portrayed by the media. This led to a conversation about whose mothers are represented and how families are usually represented as having a mother and father even if this isnt always the case in real life. One of the children made a connection to the Manitoba flood victims, saying that some of the people who lost their homes won't be able to celebrate Mothers Day. This led to brain storming what we could do to help the flood victims.	• Research using Mother's Day flyers. • (Re)creating Mothers Day flyers. • Brainstorming. • Organizing for the clothing drive. • Letter writing.	• Clothing drive.	• How do people become disadvantaged? • Who are the disadvantaged? • How are some people able to disadvantage others? • What does it mean to be privileged?

TABLE 2.2A

Chart of Artifacts Posted on Our Audit Trail

Artifact	Artifact Description	Issue(s) Addressed
	• Book cover from *Quick as a Cricket*	• environmental issues • saving the rainforest
	• Question – "Is this a frog or a toad?" • Illustration from the book *Quick as a Cricket*	• environmental issues • saving the rainforest
	• Question – "Where do these frogs live?" • Photo of toy frogs in our classroom	• environmental issues • saving the rainforest
	• Book cover from *Rainforests* • Quote – "People shouldn't cut down trees in the rainforest or frogs like this will die"	• environmental issues • saving the rainforest

TABLE 2.2B

Chart of Artifacts Posted on Our Audit Trail

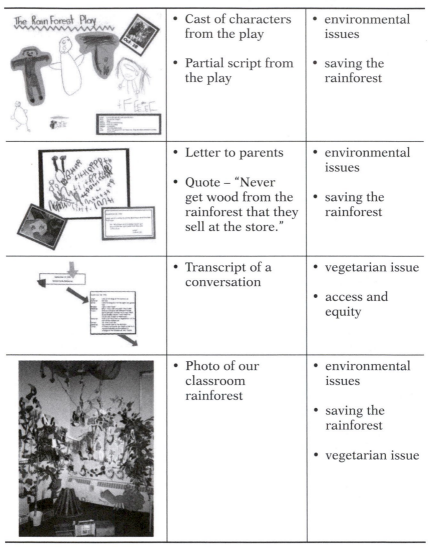

	• Cast of characters from the play • Partial script from the play	• environmental issues • saving the rainforest
	• Letter to parents • Quote – "Never get wood from the rainforest that they sell at the store."	• environmental issues • saving the rainforest
	• Transcript of a conversation	• vegetarian issue • access and equity
	• Photo of our classroom rainforest	• environmental issues • saving the rainforest • vegetarian issue

TABLE 2.2C

Chart of Artifacts Posted on Our Audit Trail

	• Quote – "Let's send it to all the wood shops. Its about wood shops not getting wood cut down from the rainforest." • Poster for wood shops • Photo of child at work	• environmental issues • saving the rainforest • responsibility
	• Photo of creating travel trunks • Page from a phone book	• environmental issues • saving the rainforest • activism
	• Photo of kids at work on travel trunks • Quote – "We make letters for the shops and mommies and daddies. We can make some for other kids too!"	• environmental issues • saving the rainforest

TABLE 2.2D
Chart of Artifacts Posted on Our Audit Trail

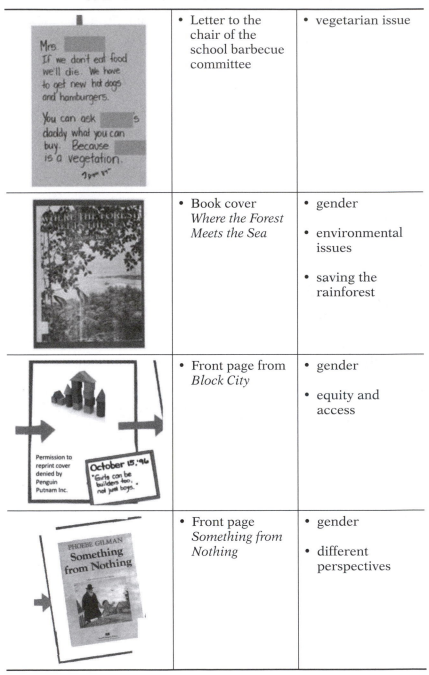

Mrs. ▮▮▮▮ If we don't eat food we'll die. We have to get new hot dogs and hamburgers. You can ask ▮▮▮▮'s daddy what you can buy. Because ▮▮▮▮ is a vegetation.	• Letter to the chair of the school barbecue committee	• vegetarian issue
	• Book cover *Where the Forest Meets the Sea*	• gender • environmental issues • saving the rainforest
Permission to reprint cover denied by Penguin Putnam Inc. October 15, '96 "Girls can be builders too, not just boys."	• Front page from *Block City*	• gender • equity and access
PHOEBE GILMAN Something from Nothing	• Front page *Something from Nothing*	• gender • different perspectives

TABLE 2.2E
Chart of Artifacts Posted on Our Audit Trail

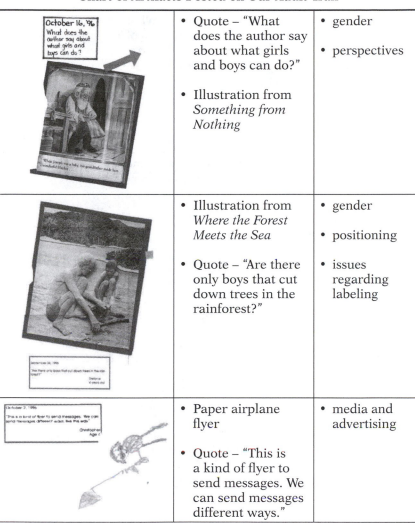

	• Quote – "What does the author say about what girls and boys can do?" • Illustration from *Something from Nothing*	• gender • perspectives
	• Illustration from *Where the Forest Meets the Sea* • Quote – "Are there only boys that cut down trees in the rainforest?"	• gender • positioning • issues regarding labeling
	• Paper airplane flyer • Quote – "This is a kind of flyer to send messages. We can send messages different ways."	• media and advertising

TABLE 2.2F

Chart of Artifacts Posted on Our Audit Trail

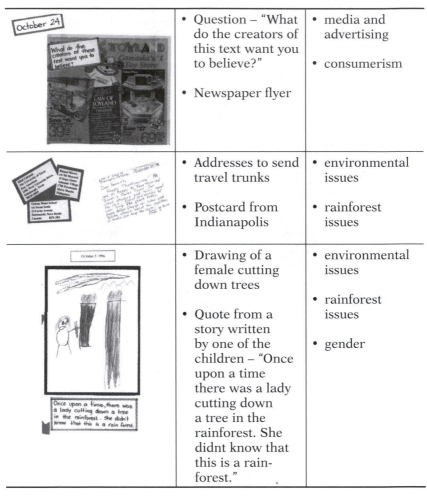

October 24	• Question – "What do the creators of this text want you to believe?" • Newspaper flyer	• media and advertising • consumerism
	• Addresses to send travel trunks • Postcard from Indianapolis	• environmental issues • rainforest issues
October 3 1996 Once upon a time, there was a lady cutting down a tree in the rainforest. She didn't know that this is a rain forest.	• Drawing of a female cutting down trees • Quote from a story written by one of the children – "Once upon a time there was a lady cutting down a tree in the rainforest. She didnt know that this is a rain-forest."	• environmental issues • rainforest issues • gender

TABLE 2.2G

Chart of Artifacts Posted on Our Audit Trail

	• Book cover of *The Great Kapok Tree* • Book cover for *Window*	• environmental issues • civics • ethical responsibility • community
	• Book cover for *Bad Egg*	• different perspectives • language and positioing
	• Drawing of Superman	• different perspectives
	• Math graph	• different perspectives • gender

TABLE 2.2H

Chart of Artifacts Posted on Our Audit Trail

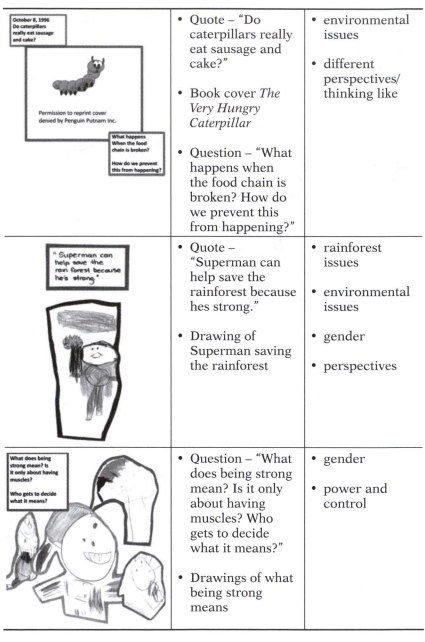

October 8, 1996 Do caterpillars really eat sausage and cake? *Permission to reprint cover denied by Penguin Putnam Inc.* What happens When the food chain is broken? How do we prevent this from happening?	• Quote – "Do caterpillars really eat sausage and cake?" • Book cover *The Very Hungry Caterpillar* • Question – "What happens when the food chain is broken? How do we prevent this from happening?"	• environmental issues • different perspectives/ thinking like
"Superman can help save the rain forest because he's strong."	• Quote – "Superman can help save the rainforest because hes strong." • Drawing of Superman saving the rainforest	• rainforest issues • environmental issues • gender • perspectives
What does being strong mean? Is it only about having muscles? Who gets to decide what it means?	• Question – "What does being strong mean? Is it only about having muscles? Who gets to decide what it means?" • Drawings of what being strong means	• gender • power and control

TABLE 2.2I
Chart of Artifacts Posted on Our Audit Trail

	• Poster of International children	• gender • perspectives and thinking like • racism • cultural issues
	• Illustrations from *Asakas Animals*	• Perspective and thinking like
	• Drawing of Spiderman from a Christmas perspective	• perspectives

TABLE 2.2J
Chart of Artifacts Posted on Our Audit Trail

	• drawings • Photos of kids at work • Quote – "If you work at it, you can be strong in your head, to write things down you never did before. That's what strong is too!"	• gender • perspectives • strength and power
	• Quote – "I learned something that I couldn't do. I can do cartwheels now." • photos	• gender • perspectives • strength and power
	• Illustrations from *Why the Willow Weeps*	• perspectives

TABLE 2.2K

Chart of Artifacts Posted on Our Audit Trail

January 8, 1997 **Different people wear different jewelry for different reasons. It means different things like money.**	• quote	• strength and power • race and culture
	• Second letter to the chair of the school barbecue committee • Response from the chair of the committee	• vegetarian issue • age equity
Dear Principal, We want to check that the vegetarians have food at the next barbecue in your school if you have one. Our friend couldn't eat at our barbecue because he is a vegetarian and that wasn't fair. Now we want to take care that all the kids can eat at the barbecue even the vegetarians.	• Letter to principals at other schools	• vegetarian issue
February 4, 1997 Maybe principals at other schools might not know about having food for vegetarians at their barbecues.	• quote	• vegetarian issue • health issues • access and fairness

TABLE 2.2L
Chart of Artifacts Posted on Our Audit Trail

	• Book cover from *Panther Dream*	• rainforest issues • environmental issues • strength and power
January 10, 1997 **Some of the things in Panther Dream are the same as our rainforest play.**	• quote	• rainforest issue
	• Text printed from a website	• rainforest issue • environmental issues
	• Graphic printed from a website	• rainforest issue • environmental issues

TABLE 2.2M

Chart of Artifacts Posted on Our Audit Trail

	• Letter to parents regarding making boxes	• age equity
January 22, Sailor Moon uses jewelry to be powerful. But for powerful you don't need jewelry. You need your brain. The people who make Sailor Moon, it's their job to make money.	• quote	• strength and power • gender • television
	• Flyer for International Women's Day contest • Bookmark Contest entry • Quote – "Women and girls are strong too!"	• strength and power • gender • age discrimination
	• survey • questionnaire • survey summary • Beluga art pieces	• environmental issues • conservation

TABLE 2.2N

Chart of Artifacts Posted on Our Audit Trail

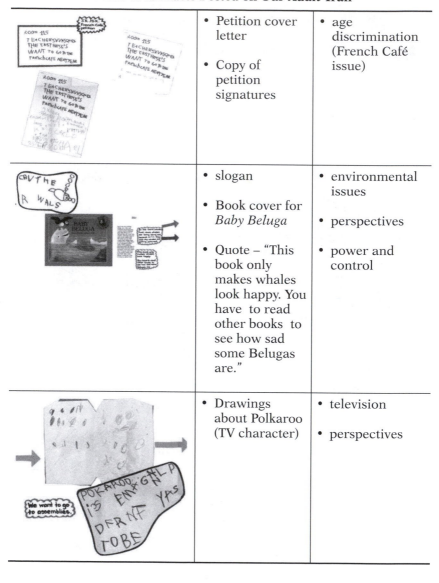

• Petition cover letter • Copy of petition signatures	• age discrimination (French Café issue)
• slogan • Book cover for *Baby Beluga* • Quote – "This book only makes whales look happy. You have to read other books to see how sad some Belugas are."	• environmental issues • perspectives • power and control
• Drawings about Polkaroo (TV character)	• television • perspectives

TABLE 2.20
Chart of Artifacts Posted on Our Audit Trail

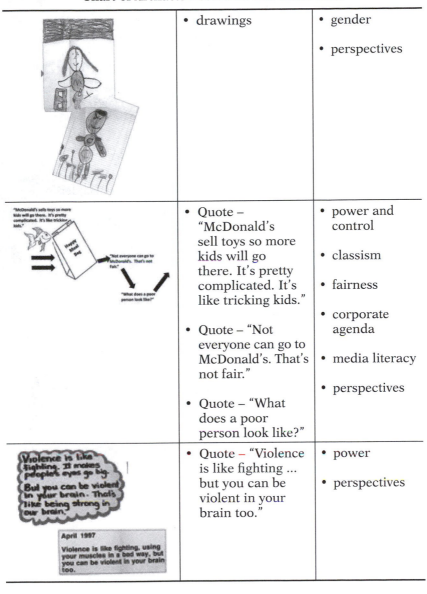

	• drawings	• gender • perspectives
	• Quote – "McDonald's sell toys so more kids will go there. It's pretty complicated. It's like tricking kids." • Quote – "Not everyone can go to McDonald's. That's not fair." • Quote – "What does a poor person look like?"	• power and control • classism • fairness • corporate agenda • media literacy • perspectives
	• Quote – "Violence is like fighting ... but you can be violent in your brain too."	• power • perspectives

TABLE 2.2P

Chart of Artifacts Posted on Our Audit Trail

	• Book cover from *Crafty Chameleon* • Quote from the book	• strength and power • perspectives
	• quote • drawings	• gender • perspectives
	• Question – "What about Mothers Day?" • quotes	• fairness • culture • perspectives • Manitoba flood
	• Invitations for speakers • conference booklet	• age equity • vegetarian issue • animal rights • gender

TABLE 2.2Q

Chart of Artifacts Posted on Our Audit Trail

	• poster • donation letter	• helping others in need (Manitoba flood victims) • civics
What next year's JK-3 should know Listen to the other kids Remember other people's feelings If there's something happening in the school and you want to go, you can make something like petitions. Boys and girls should share their feelings and talk and not fight. You have to share with the other kids Put things away after you use them You can be strong from your brain You should know that McDonalds and the newspaper and books and schools can make you think their way.	• Poster for next year's Junior Kindergartens (what they should know)	• general • community
room 15 YE YANT To HAV PLAY DAY YETH ALOF ALSALNTS	• Draft of petition cover letter regarding attending play day with the rest of the school	• age discrimination • power and control
May 27, 1997 The Power Rangers show changed again because kids could get bored. The people who make the show change it so kids will keep watching.	• drawing • quote regarding • Power Rangers	• power and control • gender • media • corporate agenda

TABLE 2.2R
Chart of Artifacts Posted on Our Audit Trail

I know how to play pin ball. Some people say it's a boys game. It's up to us girls to tell boys what we can do.	• quote	• gender
May 29, 1997 That's like McDonalds. Sometimes they even decide what boys and girls are supposed to be like. That's like when they gave girls Barbies and toy cars.	• quote	• gender • corporate agenda

Deciding on What Incidents to Represent on Our Audit Trail

There are many incidents that are represented on our audit trail. At the same time, there were several other incidents that were not included. However, this is not to say that some incidents were significant and others were not. As we worked through various critical incidents and issues, the children and I made decisions about what to post. The impact an issue had in the social worlds of the children or the kind of contribution to change in our social spaces determined what was posted. Often, children wanted to post artifacts of incidents that they took the most pleasure in pursuing. We decided on what these were primarily based on what the children said during our class meetings. How much time the children wanted to devote to a topic also signaled their level of pleasure with exploring that topic. Deciding on what incidents to include on our audit trail and the artifacts to represent those incidents happened during class meeting.

Visibly Connecting Issues on Our Audit Trail

Connecting issues on our audit trail happened in two ways. First, as artifacts were posted on the wall, we began to talk about how different incidents could be part of a broader underlying issue. Based on these connections, we identified six overarching themes:

1. *Environmental Issues*. Environmental issues were issues that dealt in some way with the environment, such as harvesting rain forests or what happens when forested areas are cleared to make room for building houses.
2. *Different People and Different Places*. Issues connected to this theme were issues of diversity or difference, whether this was based on, for example, ethnicity or income.
3. *Girls and Boys*. The girls and boys theme had to do with any incidents that dealt with issues of gender equity.
4. *TV and Newspapers*. This particular theme looked at the role that media played in socializing children and influencing who they could and could not be in the world.
5. *Strength and Power*. Strength and power dealt with issues of control and marginalization, disadvantage, privilege, and oppression.
6. *Thinking Like*. This theme dealt with incidents where we looked at issues or topics from different perspectives.

These themes were highlighted and posted on our audit trail in consecutive order. For example, the environmental issues theme was the first theme to be highlighted. I cut out large round pieces of construction paper on which to print the various themes. The children called these circles "hot spots" because "they look like the sun" (Fig. 2.12).

In order to represent the connections between the various issues and to highlight the themes identified, I cut out arrows from different colors of construction paper. I used a particular color to represent a particular theme. For example, orange arrows represented gender issues and yellow arrows represented environmental issues. These arrows were then stapled between artifacts on our audit trail to show how issues were connected (Fig. 2.13). Different colored arrows that converged on an artifact visually represented how different themes were connected. For example, Fig. 2.14 illustrates how a conversation about the near extinction of beluga whales in the St. Lawrence River in Canada concerned issues dealing with the environment, age equity, media, and different perspectives. This particular issue was originally taken up as an environmental issue and animal rights issue. One of the children had seen a television documentary about the pollution in the St. Lawrence River that resulted

FIG. 2.12.   Hot Spots.

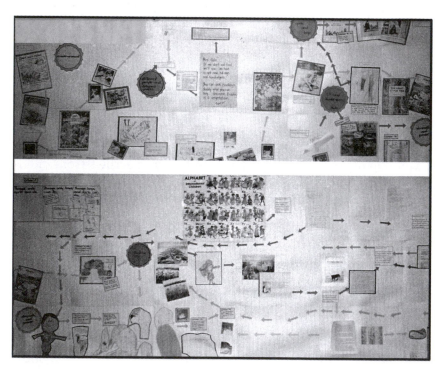

FIG. 2.13.   Arrows Connecting Issues on Our Audit Trail.

FIG. 2.14. Converging Arrows on Our Audit Trail.

in the poisoning of beluga whales. The issue of age equity came into play as the children talked about how, in spite of their young age, they could find ways to support the plight of the beluga whales. A conversation about media came up as we talked about how the media could be used to help inform the public about the issue and how the issue has been represented in the media. For example, how were the activists portrayed? Were they portrayed as people attempting to do some good or radical people who like to cause trouble? We also talked about how this issue was an important one and yet none of us had noticed anything written about it in newspapers or television news reports. In terms of different perspectives, we talked about how a person's stance on life issues would dictate the kind of action or inaction that one might take regarding problems such as the near extinction of the beluga whales (see Chapter 5).

Critical Literacy Across the Curriculum

Another curricular connection made visible through the use of the audit trail is the way that the work we did cut across the

TABLE 2.3
Critical Literacy Across the Curriculum: The Beluga Study

Curricular Area	Activity
Science	• animal life (marine mammals) • endangered species
Social Studies	• civic engagement • Geography • mapping
Language Arts	• reading • writing • researching • explaining
Mathematics	• The Beluga Store • economics • counting • money • measurement
Music	• re-writing the Beluga song • performing the song
Arts	• role playing at the Beluga store • creating art pieces focused on Beluga whales

disciplines. The previous chart (Table 2.3) is an example of the cross-curricular work we accomplished during our inquiry about the beluga whale. For instance, the work on contributing to protecting the beluga whales started out as a social studies (civic engagement, geography) and science (animal life, endangered species) activity. Rewriting the beluga song was a music, drama, and language arts activity, and then the work done on the Save the Beluga store involved math and economics.

The Audit Trail: Assessment and Evaluation

Murphy (2003) notes that the assessment tool used determines the nature of the literacy that is produced. For instance, a literacy curriculum that values the use of a standardized test, which focuses heavily on phonological awareness out of context, can be said to value phonics as a deterministic activity. What this means is that how well a child does on this standardized test is used to determine how well he or she is doing with regard to literacy learning. Such assessments are often associated with the "increased governance and oversight of early childhood education" (Murphy, 2003, p. 565) that is becoming increasingly widespread. Research has shown, however, that such assessments are not sufficient because what we learn most about children is how well they do on the particular test they are given. We do not necessarily learn about what they know and how they come to know what they know, which are crucial pieces of information that teachers need to construct a curriculum that has children as the central concern.

Murphy (2003) notes, "escaping the discourse of determinative judgment is difficult" (p. 569). The good news is that alternate visions are available, such as the reflective assessments that take the form of pedagogical documentation used in Reggio Emilia schools (Guidici, Rinaldi, & Krechevsky, 2001; Rinaldi, 2004). Rinaldi (2004) asks the following types of questions with regard to this type of assessment:

- How can we help children to make sense of their experiences?
- How can we as teachers make sense of our students' experiences?

According to Rinaldi (2004), the whole point of pedagogical documentation is to come up with an interpretive theory or a narration that gives meaning to events and objects of the world (pp. 79–80). Murphy (2003) notes that with the use of this kind of assessment, "the assessor who in determinative assessment, stands somewhat apart from the work of learning to place value on it, is replaced by a child and adult who conjointly work to find value by theorizing and coming to understand the experiences gestured to in the documentation" (p. 569). Therefore, this is not observation as surveillance to see if teachers have done their jobs and to see if children's performances match what is on the mandated checklist (Genishi & Haas Dyson, 2009). "Rather it is observation that leads to learning more about children's knowledge and know-how in particular situations and to helping them learn more"(Genishi & Haas Dyson, 2009, p. 118).

Traditional documentation often happens at the end of the learning process as summative proof or evidence that learning has taken place and as a tool for judging teaching. This type of documentation is most useful for teachers, parents, and administrators responsible for observing the work of teachers. In contrast, creating an audit trail is an ongoing documentative process that makes learning visible and allows children and their teachers, along with parents, guardians, and others involved in the child's schooling, to retrace their thinking throughout their yearlong learning journey. This learning, which takes place over time, is referred to by Genishi and Haas Dyson as "part of each child's assessment timeline" (p. 118). In a way, the artifacts created and/or collected and posted on the audit trail make visible the world(s) children live in both in and out of school as well as their in-and-out-of-school identities (Pahl & Rowsell, 2010). Rinaldi (2004) notes that when learning is made visible as in the use of the audit trail, which includes real examples of children's work, words or actions, we always gain insight into what is on the children's minds as well as insight into their potential.

The Audit Trail and Standards of Learning

In an educational system driven by standards, the audit trail can be "mined for evidence of the benchmarks identified by school governance systems" (Murphy, 2003, p. 570) rather than using those benchmarks or standards as the basis for constructing curriculum. As presented in Chapter 1, when I reflected on the narrative of learning depicted in the audit trail, it quickly became evident to me that the work we were doing produced cross-curricular literacies that surpassed the mandated curriculum that was in place at our school! The same would be true for any mandated or core curriculum to which teachers are made accountable. For instance, the Common Core Kindergarten English Language Arts Strand lists the following standards for Presentation of Knowledge and Ideas:

- Describe familiar people, places, things, and events and, with prompting and support, provide additional detail.
- Add drawings or other visual displays to descriptions as desired to provide additional detail.
- Speak audibly and express thoughts, feelings, and ideas clearly. (Common Core State Standards Initiative, 2012)

In the next three chapters, which are demonstrations of possibilities for critical literacies, you will see how the work we did created opportunities for the children to readily describe the world around them without prompting. They did this because the work we did had significance in their lives. This was inevitable given that the curriculum was negotiated using their inquiry questions and topics that were on their minds. The audit trail itself was a visual display of learning and thinking over time. Any visitor to our classroom was welcomed with a walkthrough of our learning wall. The children became very good at articulating the events posted on our wall as well as the connections between each of the events. They also readily shared the significance of each of the artifacts on the audit trail. Clearly, the work that we did surpassed the standards previously listed. As such, building curriculum strictly from those standards would in fact have negated potentially rich learning experiences.

With regard to standards, what I often tell my teacher education students is that they need to know what is being asked of them so that they can create the spaces they need to do work such as critical literacies. This also makes it easier for them to find evidence in the work they are doing to show they have in fact either addressed various issues or topics in the mandated documents or that they have surpassed what was being asked.

Alternate Possibilities for Constructing an Audit Trail

Since the first edition of this book was published, many educators have taken on the idea of creating an audit trail in their settings with learners of varying ages. What I like about the examples is that they offer other possible ways for constructing an audit trail. Some of them have even shared their work with me. For instance, Faige Meller used photographs in creating a "Learning Trail" with her kindergarten students. She wrote the following:

Dear Vivian,

I am a kindergarten teacher at an Independent co-educational day school in West Hollywood. We have approximately 540 students, Early Childhood (Toddlers) through 6th Grade. We are a socio-economically and culturally diverse population (49% students of color, 16% of students receive financial aid). Our faculty works in a team-teaching model: each elementary classroom has two master credentialed teachers.

*After learning about the audit trail in your book "Nego-
tiating Critical Literacies with Young Children," I
thought it would be a wonderful way for my students to
reflect on their learning throughout the year. Each month
we added interesting pictures to the "Learning Trail" and
had discussions about events and themes presented. For
example, when learning about our Olympic Countries,
artifacts pertaining to each country were displayed and
then photographed for our trail. Evidence of the children
working, from building cities with blocks to creating art
in outdoor spaces . . . was documented in photographs
for the audit trail. In June as we looked forward to our
Kindergarten Graduation, the children had many opportunities to look at their "Learning Trail" and review with
each other and the teachers the salient and exciting
experiences in their kindergarten year. This helped them
recall some of their favorite memories. Throughout the
year, when you entered our room, you would often find
a teacher taking pictures of enthusiastic kindergarten
children wanting to be captured with their cherished
work. In that way our trail expanded in the direction that
the class chose; it was one that I had not anticipated but
that was truly meaningful. This was authentic learning
propelled by my "kinders!" All of this was contained on
one bulletin board. Next year holds further promise of a
"Learning (audit) Trail" inspired by the children's wonders, interests and design of their own learning.*

Similarly, Minda Morren Lopez, a professor at Texas State University made use of audit trails in the preservice (undergraduate)
courses in literacy that she was teaching. The two courses were
field-based courses for juniors and seniors that integrate literacy
theory and methods with an internship in a classroom. The university courses were taught at a public elementary school campus twice
a week where the preservice teachers interned in a classroom twice
a week. What she did was to ask her students to create their own
audit trails using Web 2.0 technologies. They tried two different sites

for this work (www.dipity.com or www.capzles.com) before finally deciding on using Prezi. (www.prezi.com)

In the course syllabus she wrote,

> This semester we will use audit trails to keep track of our learning. Each of you will create your own audit trail online (choose from several options for creating the audit trail) and we will also create a whole class audit trail. We will share our audit trails periodically in class and there will be "checkpoints" throughout the semester—dates where you need to have a certain number of entries.

Figure 2.15a and Figure 2.15b are examples of the audit trails created in Minda's class.

Aby's Audit Trail
http://prezi.com/xutkyuo7br0b/abys-audit-trail/

Clicking on the different virtual artifacts results in zooming in on that particular artifact so that you get a close up look at what has been posted.

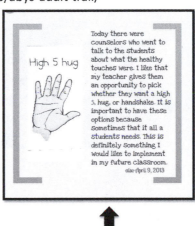

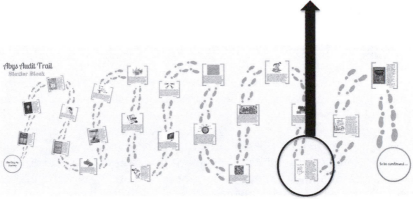

FIG. 2.15a & b   Virtual Audit Trail Example 1 & 2.

Paul's Audit Trail
http://prezi.com/np-sgzk7jcgd/my-journey/

Clicking on the different virtual artifacts results in zooming in on that particular artifact so that you get a close up look at what has been posted.

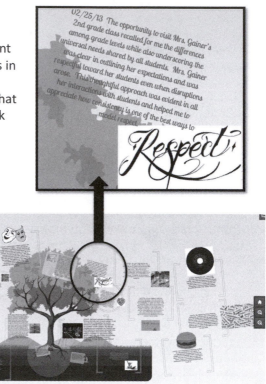

FIG. 2.15a & b. (Continued)

Minda noted that how students chose artifacts was entirely up to them. She tried to guide them by telling them to choose aha moments that they had while reading and/or interacting with students and teachers at the school. She also encouraged them to think and reflect on learning they thought would impact them the most as future teachers.

Upon reflecting on the use of audit trails, Minda wrote, "I think the audit trails helped the students think about more specific learning experiences and reflect more about what they were learning in the classes and their intern experiences. I also think it helped to connect students to each other and create more of a community."

What I love about these two examples is that they demonstrate the use of an audit trail with both children and adults. The examples also show the range of potential ways of constructing an audit trail by using photographs as Faige did with her young students and by using software such as Prezi as Minda did with her teacher education students. In Appendix B, I have included a number of other ideas for creating audit trails in various settings. However, regardless of what age group of students you may be working with, the audit trail can be a useful and powerful tool for teaching, learning, and reflecting, as previously noted.

In the next four chapters (3–6), I take you on a closer look at a series of incidents represented on our class audit trail that led to particular critical studies and social action. Each of these chapters begins with a section to contextualize the incident and is followed by a series of subsections that describe what happened. It is in this part of each chapter that I offer my analysis. Finally, at the end of each chapter, I include critical reflections and pedagogical questions for you to consider.

3

The French Café

Setting the Scene

At the time of my teacher research study, French was a mandatory second language subject taught to students between the ages of 6 and 13 in Ontario, Canada. This mandate stems from the Official Languages Act of 1985. The purposes for the Act include ensuring respect for English and French as the official languages of Canada, supporting the development of English and French linguistic minority communities, and generally advancing the equality of status and use of the English and French languages within Canadian society. Historically, during the 1600s and 1700s, Canada was fought over by the British and French and was therefore occupied by the British and the French at different points in time.

As a result of the Official Languages Act, the government of Ontario mandated French to be taught to children starting in first grade. Some schools in Ontario also offer French Immersion programs where French is the primary language of instruction. At our school, the French Café was an offshoot of the mandated French curriculum. Those who attend the café are served fruit juice and croissants. The rationale for hosting a café was to give the students in seventh and eighth grade an opportunity to practice their French while running the café. Because French is not a mandatory subject for Junior Kindergarten and Senior Kindergarten students, they generally do not participate in the French Café. There is much to be addressed regarding French as an imposed curriculum, in light of the growing number of ethnic groups and thus second and third languages spoken by different ethnic communities in Ontario, Canada. In our class, for example, nine ethnicities are represented, none of which is French. However, at the time of this inquiry, a different issue took center stage: the equitable participation of young children in school events.

What Is a French Café?

It is 9AM, time for morning announcements. Although the children and I somewhat quiet down, just in case something of pertinence to us is shared over the public announcement system, the children continue with a buzz of learning. Any observer might note that they do not seem at all interested in what is being shared over what the children have dubbed "the school radio station." This morning, however, was a little different as the principal welcomed guests to the day's special event, the annual French Café.

"What's a French Café?" some of the children asked. "Well, it's like a restaurant set up by some of the older children in our school, for one day," I answered. "Why did he say, 'Welcome guests'?" the children asked. Curtis spoke up from the doorway of our classroom, "Look, where are they all going? To the café? Those are the guests that he's saying welcome to!" He was referring to the trickling of parents and guardians who had come to our school to attend the café. "Who else is going to this?" he continued. Intent on finding an answer to his question, he stood at the door and kept track of who was making their way to the gymnasium where the café was being staged. When he thought he had observed enough, he called a class meeting to share his hypothesis that he thought most everyone, but some younger kids, would make their way to the café at some point during the day. "I think that because I already saw older kids and younger kids, and mommies and daddies and babysitters going to the café," he concluded. "You think all the kids are going, Curtis?" one of the other children asked. Suddenly, he remembered that his brother, who is in first grade, had mentioned something about going to the café. With this, Curtis returned to what became his observation post for the day, our classroom doorway, to wait for evidence of the Grade 1 classes attending the café. He had made an observation sheet (see Fig. 3.1), which he used to track who was going to the café. The observation sheet consisted of a row of numbers representing each grade level.

As each group of students walked past our door toward the café, he asked them what grade they were in and then he placed a check mark beside their corresponding grade level on his observation sheet (see Fig. 3.2). "The grade ones are coming, the grade ones are coming!" he excitedly announced. "So that means the grade ones

FIG. 3.1. French Café Survey Form.

FIG. 3.2. Curtis' French Café Observation Sheet.

are going, the grade twos are going, the grade threes are going . . . everyone is going."

"Why can't we go? Who else can't go?" he asked, and then said, "If we had Grade 13 they would probably go too!" "Can I ask if the other Kindergartens and the other Junior Kindergarten class is going?" he continued. Seeing me nod my head in agreement, he quickly asked a couple of the other children to go with him. Upon their return, the three children called an emergency class meeting to share the information they had gathered. It was at this time that the following discussion took place.

1 Curtis:	Okay, the two kindergarten classes are NOT going and the other Junior Kindergarten class is NOT going and we are NOT going!	
2 Melanie:	This is impossible.	
3 Teacher:	Then what is possible? How can we change what's possible?	
4 Curtis:	Maybe we can make a survey to see how much of each kids want to go.	
5 Stefanie:	Yes, let's find out from the other kindergartens.	
6 Lee:	If more people want to go then next year maybe they'll let us go.	
7 Curtis:	Can we tape that it's not fair?	
8 Teacher:	At our Speaker's Corner?	
9 Melanie:	That's a good idea. Then, we can send the tape of us talking so they'll know that we want to go.	
10 Tiffany:	Yea, we think it's not fair.	
11 Curtis:	Who wants to do a survey?	
12 Teacher:	Tell me about your survey.	
13 Curtis:	We'll ask all the kindergartens and junior kindergartens yes or no, do you want to go to the French Café?	
14 Melanie:	You did that already.	
15 P.J.:	We didn't answer yes or no.	
16 Curtis:	We just didn't do a writing one.	
17 Tiffany:	We just said SAY, SAY if you want to.	
18 Melanie:	Right. Not sign yes or no, just SAY, but we could still do a writed out one.	
19 Teacher:	What reason could you give for doing that?	
20 Melanie & Curtis:	So we'll know.	

21 Teacher: What information do you think the written infor-
               mation will give you that you don't already have?
22 Tiffany: Like a different answer?
23 P.J.:   Everyone will still say yes. I will . . .
24 Curtis: So we won't find out new stuff. We already
               know what we'll find out?
25 Melanie: Yup, we know what we want to find out about
               already.
26 Teacher: Who were you planning giving the survey to?
27 Curtis: Just for us to find out how many people want to
               and so we can tell the people who is the chair
               of the French Café.
28 Teacher: I have a suggestion for another way to pass on
               information to the French Café organizers. I
               think that maybe a petition might be a way to
               show that many of us, maybe most of the JKs
               and SKs might feel the same way.
29 Curtis: Do we get everyone to write letters to them?
30 Teacher: Sort of but that would take a long time. What
               I'm thinking about is called a petition. Instead
               of asking a question for people to answer, you
               write out what you are thinking and then have
               people sign their name after it.
31 Melanie: Then what happens?
32 Tiffany: Then we bring it to the chair?
33 P.J.:   Why lots of names and one letter?
34 Teacher: Well you don't really need a lot of letters in this
               case, especially because they would all be say-
               ing pretty well the same thing. What you would
               do is to ask people who agree with you to sign
               it. The more names you have, the stronger your
               petition is!
35 Curtis: Oh, that's like one brain is strong but lots of
               brains is stronger!

After our class meeting, different groups of children began
working on their various tasks. Curtis and a group of three other
children, soon to be known as the French Café Petition Committee,
wrote a cover letter for the petition (see Fig. 3.3). A copy of the letter
was attached to a blank sheet of paper and delivered to each of the
other Junior Kindergarten (JK) and Kindergarten (SK) classrooms.

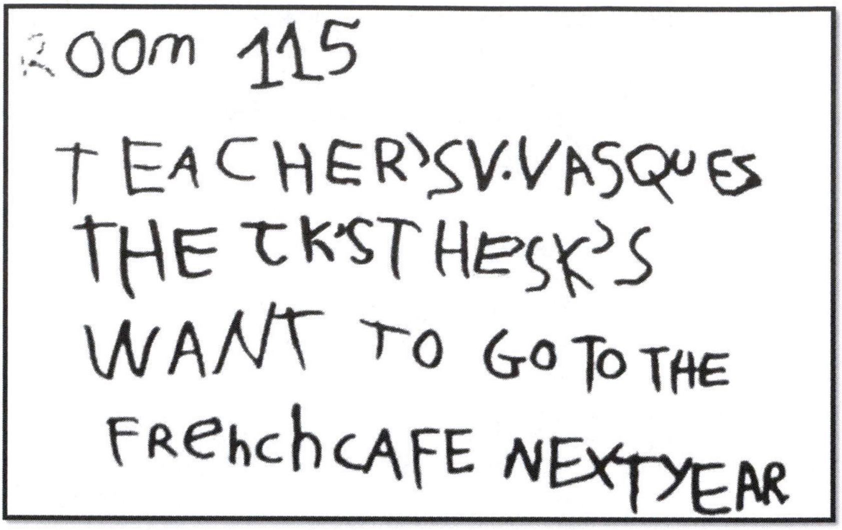

> ℛOOm 115
>
> TEACHER'SV.VASQUES
> THE TK'STHE'SK'S
> WANT TO GO TO THE
> FRehchCAFE NEXTYEAR

FIG. 3.3.   French Café Petition Letter.

The children explained the reason for the petition to the other classes and arranged to collect it the following school day.

The next day, the children eagerly entered the classroom, excited about going to the other JK and SK classes to gather the signed petitions. During class meeting, the committee shared the results of the petition, showing the class a list of names that had been produced and reporting on the total number of signatures that had been gathered. At the same time, another group of children began working on a Speaker's Corner tape to be delivered with the petition to strengthen their case (see Fig. 3.4 and Fig. 3.5). In Ontario, the "Speaker's Corner" was a well-known segment in a television program carried by the local station. Segments aired on the TV show are taken from video recordings created by the general public at the Speaker's Corner booth located outside the station. Anyone who wanted to air his or her views or talk on a particular issue or topic could do so for $2. The setup was similar to the photo booths that can be found in various shopping malls. A number of these recordings were then selected and played on national television at various times during evening programming. The idea for a Speaker's Corner was therefore well known to many of my students.

Constructing a Speaker's Corner in our classroom came up as a result of some children having viewed these segments on television. Audiotaping our thinking or conversations was one way that

FIG. 3.4.   Our Class Speaker's Corner.

we thought we could represent and later revisit various things that had come up as issues in the classroom. Our Speaker's Corner consisted of a tape recorder, audio cassettes, and a place to display or hold our recordings.

Today there's something going on in the gym
and we want to know why aren't we invited?
Because only the grade ones and twos can go so
that's not fair to us or to anyone.

And maybe (on the next on the, maybe on the
next party, maybe) on the next party we can
have it at our class.

But we figured out something. If we have
dances here then they won't have dances there
and if they have dances there we won't have
dances here. And that's not fair to us or to the
whole world because we don't get to go.

Maybe they don't understand.

Or maybe they think that we're bored or that
we're not old enough but we are not going to be
bored if we were even invited.

So, this is a French Cafe and we hope that we
can go next year.

Thank you.

FIG. 3.5.   Transcript of French Café Speaker's Corner Tape.

The children were able to record at our Speaker's Corner at any time during the day. Often, topics shared at Speaker's Corner originate from discussion that takes place during our class meetings or while children are engaged in small group work. On occasion, children came to school having thought about what they wanted to record at our Speaker's Corner.

Analyzing the French Café

Knowledge is never neutral or said differently; everything we know is socially constructed. According to Fiske (1989), "knowledge is power and its circulation is part of the social distribution of power." (p. 149). So children need opportunities to learn the relationship between the circulation of knowledge through language use and the power associated with certain forms of language (Comber,

1999). The action taken by my students toward being included in school functions such as the French Café is one way to raise concern about the existing power structure where young children are not treated as equal participants in the school community. The work toward the action the children took offered a space in which to change how they were positioned in the social hierarchy of school: in whole language terms, to give them a voice so that they are able to participate differently.

When Curtis asked his initial question, "Why can't we go?" I could have responded in one of three ways:

1. Explaining that the French Café is only for those children who are taking French, or that the French Café is only for the older students.
2. Reposing the question, asking, "Why do you think we aren't invited?"
3. Offering a critical challenge, asking, "What can we do to change the situation?"

In relation to Curtis' question—"Why can't we go?"—the first response possibility, explaining that the French Café is only for the older children, treats his question as a fact with a potentially uncritical but valid answer. The second response possibility, reposing the question, positions Curtis a little differently but can easily lead toward responding to his question with an activity. For example, I could have sent him off to come up with some ideas as to why things are the way they are and then I would have talked to him about his findings without necessarily taking social action. The third response possibility, offering a critical challenge, treats Curtis' question as an opportunity for taking social action, disrupting inequity, and changing the way in which my students could participate in the school event and beyond. What results are critical literacies as Curtis took on the role of researching his world asking why things are the way they are.

The hypothesis that inexplicably the Junior Kindergartens and Kindergartens were the only groups not invited to the French Café was arrived at systematically as Curtis engaged in observational research (Fig. 3.2) and through class discussion (lines 1–35). In her account of the social worlds of children learning to write, Dyson (1993) talks about how children nudge the bounds of the official imaginative universe that prevails in schools. In doing so, they challenge current theoretical and pedagogical thinking. She said they do this while participating in the complicated world of school. In the same way, Curtis and the French Café Petition Committee nudged the bounds as they repositioned the Junior and Senior Kindergarten children as equal participants in life at our school. In doing so, they moved toward an alternate possibility, not only considering a different school world but also creating an opportunity for change. As a result of the children's action, the Junior and Senior Kindergarten students were included in future Cafés. The petition and Speaker's Corner tape met with little resistance from other teachers. I think this response stemmed in part from surprise at the children's action and in part from seeing these young children differently. Through taking social action, the children learned not only a different way to resist, participate in community, and exercise their democratic abilities; they also learned of the possibilities available through collectively working through a problem.

Learning About Powerful Forms of Language

The conversation on finding out what the other kindergartens thought led to a discussion regarding the difference between a survey and a petition.

> 4 Curtis: Maybe we can make a survey to see how much of each kids want to go.
> 5 Stefanie: Yes, let's find out from the other kindergartens.

As a result, we began to talk about different ways of using language and the forms these could take. Once we decided that a petition was what was needed, the creation of the petition began. The children felt that having the support of the other kindergarten classes might help their attempts at being included in future French Cafés (line 35). This would also be an example of solidarity. They demonstrated their understanding of the power associated with written language as they made a case for representing what they hoped would be consensus on paper (lines 13 through 27). In their words, just "saying" (line 17) does not get the job done, but doing a "writed out" one just might work (line 18).

In order to represent the French Café action on our audit trail, we decided to post a copy of the signed petitions and cover letter (Fig. 3.6).

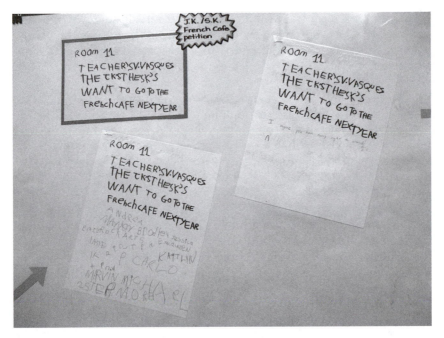

FIG. 3.6. Artifacts Representing the French Café Incident on Our Audit Trail.

Offering Children Alternate Ways of Acting

Bourdieu (1993) talked about certain forms of language use as carrying more or less cultural capital. That is the value given to certain ways of doing things in particular settings based on what is seen as most appropriate in that setting. For example, my students were certainly aware of the cultural capital that print carried in our school, and which kinds of texts and uses of language are more conducive to getting done those things that matter. By naming the form of writing under discussion as being a petition, I was simultaneously affirming that a petition was a strategy sufficiently known to the community being addressed, in this case the School French Café Committee. The strategy (petition) was therefore seen as one that has more cultural capital for the particular context in which it was used than the original survey that the children had initially suggested. My role was not to tell the children what to think or how to act, but based on their inquiries, to offer alternate ways of taking action and a way of naming their world within the stance they chose to take. In the words of the editors of *Rethinking Schools* (Bigelow, Christensen, Karp, Miner, & Peterson, 1994),

> We want students to come to see themselves as change makers. If we ask the children to critique the world but then fail to encourage them to act, our classrooms can degenerate into factories of cynicism. While it's not a teacher's role to direct students to particular organizations, it is a teacher's role to suggest that ideas need to be acted upon and to offer students opportunities to do just that. (p. 5)

Being able to engage with critical literacies calls for questioning the existing school definition of community. The action taken by these Junior Kindergarten children raises concern with the existing power structure that treats kindergarten students as innocent neutral beings to be readied for the real world of school, that is, for first grade and the grades that follow.

According to Comber and Kamler (1997), a critical perspective offers teachers a way to think about what students are learning to read and write, what they do with that reading and writing, and what that reading and writing does to them and their world. Through engagement in a critical curriculum, my students and I raised various social justice and equity issues, using them to interrogate, obstruct, contest, and/or change inequitable situations.

In the next chapter, I describe what came to be known as the "Vegetarian Issue" where I capitalized on my students' concerns with a particular social practice at our school to work on critical language awareness.

Critical Reflections and Pedagogical Questions

At the time when the French Café took place, access to new communication technologies was somewhat limited to the use of machines such as cassette recorders and film cameras. In our classroom, we were fortunate to have had three old computers. Unfortunately, they were of the type that made use of 8-inch floppy disks that would likely be unrecognizable to young children today. As such, there was not too much we could really do with those machines. And yet I believe my students worked and played skillfully to produce texts and perform literate identities in ways that pushed them as literacy learners (Wohlwend, 2011) allowing them to participate differently in their school community.

Today we can tell a different story. Imagine what more we could have done to make public the issues we were raising. Rather than using a cassette recorder, we could have created YouTube videos (www.youtube.com/) or iMovies (www.apple.com/ca/ilife/imovie/) to which viewers could have responded with feedback, questions, and/or comments. This would have created a space for my students to connect with other children who may also be engaging in social actions projects in their settings. Children in other locations could have learned from our experiences as well. In terms of creating surveys, we could have used DoodlePoll (www.doodle.com/) or SurveyMonkey (www.surveymonkey.com/), which would have allowed us to learn about whether Junior and Senior Kindergarten students in other settings were included or excluded from school community events to further reflect on the experience of young children and their opportunities for participating in school events. For each of these possibilities, you would have to decide on how private or public these texts would be. If you are concerned regarding safety or privacy issues, you could always create and post on private sites or channels.

Following are some questions for you to consider:

- In your setting, what are some underlying issues that your students may be grappling with or topics for which they have passion?
- In your setting, what school events are promoted? For whom are these events created? Who gets to participate in those events? Are there any populations for whom any of the events are not accessible?
- What are some takeaways from the French Café incident that might inform how you might deal with your students' issues or passions?
- What might new communication technologies afford the work that you do?

4

Our Friend Is a Vegetarian

Setting the Scene

The school barbecue is an annual event for parents, children, and teachers to get together and "build school spirit." The incident that I am about to describe took place the day after the school barbecue when 4-year-old Anthony told our class, during meeting time, that he was a vegetarian and that he was not able to eat the all-beef hamburgers and hot dogs at the school barbecue.

We Have Vegetarians at Our School?

As the children came into the classroom, the air was filled with excitement about the school barbecue that took place the night before. They talked about whom they saw and what they ate. They talked about bringing their leftover potato chips and soda to school and argued over whether this was a healthy snack. Wanting to talk more about the school barbecue, Stefanie added the topic to the agenda for our class meeting. When her name was called out, she started by saying that she was interested to know whether there were more people who ate hamburgers or more people who ate hot dogs. To do this, she stated that she was "going to do a hand-count survey."

A quiet whisper could be heard from the back of the group followed by what seemed to be agitated conversation. Anthony, one of the boys in the class, had said to some of the children sitting beside him that he didn't eat at the barbecue because he is vegetarian and therefore he could not participate in Stefanie's survey.

We had been engaged in an inquiry about rain forests at the time of the barbecue and had talked about the need to preserve the rain forests so that animals and people that live there would have food and shelter. We had also talked about whose interests are served and who profits and benefits from materials harvested from rain forests. For example, we discussed how multinational companies like McDonald's, in the past, contributed to destroying rain forests by hiring suppliers who rear beef cattle on ex-rain forest land in South and Central America, thereby preventing its regeneration.

Problematizing Social Text

The children were upset that no one had thought about having food for vegetarians at the barbecue and that no one had asked if there were vegetarians in our school community. The issue became a topic of concern at a number of class meetings. During one conversation, Stefanie asked, "Who decided that we would only have beef hamburgers and hot dogs at the barbecue?" I explained that there was a committee, a group of parents and teachers that organized the barbecue, and the chair of the committee was the assistant to the principal. Apparently, Stefanie had talked about the vegetarian issue with her family, and her mom had encouraged her to investigate further. In conversation with some of the other children, it was revealed that many of them had also talked about this issue with their families.

Led by Stefanie, the group decided to act on their concern and problematize the marginalization of vegetarians at our annual school barbecue. We started by reading the announcement flyer that the children took home advertising the school barbecue. "Join us for our Annual School Barbecue" was the first line of text. "The invitation says our but doesn't really mean Anthony so it's yours and mine (pointing to other children who are not vegetarian and herself) but not his (pointing to Anthony) and that's not fair," Melanie commented. We had done some analysis of the words used in magazine ads and how pronouns work to position readers in particular ways. Here, Melanie was applying the same discursive analytic strategy using a piece of everyday text, the annual barbecue flyer.

The children agreed to have Stefanie write a letter to the chair of the school barbecue committee expressing our concern. While drafting this letter, Stefanie had a number of discussions with a group of four other children to decide what words to use. "Why don't you say that people need food to live," Melanie suggested. "And, ummm, if you don't eat, you'll die," P.J. added. "Should I say 'have to' like it's very important?" Stefanie asked. After this discussion, Stefanie asked me if I would scribe the letter. She said that we needed to send it right away and that if she had to do drafts, then it might take too long. The letter was written as follows:

If we don't eat food we'll die.
We have to get new hot dogs
and hamburgers.
You can ask Anthony's daddy
what you can buy because
Anthony is a vegetarian.

Stefanie began her letter by declaring, "If we don't eat food we'll die." The use of *we* as opposed to "If Anthony doesn't eat he'll die" was a deliberate choice based on a previous conversation about why a petition is a better tool for making a case for yourself than a survey (see The French Café, Chapter 3). Curtis, one of the boys in the class, had concluded our discussion about petitions by saying, "One brain is strong but lots of brains is stronger." When I asked Stefanie why she chose *we* over *Anthony*, she referred directly to Curtis' statement, saying, "Remember Ms. Vasquez . . . about lots of brains?" The use of *we*, therefore, is used to symbolize strength in numbers, solidarity, and inclusiveness, while in essence directing the organizer of the school barbecue and suggesting that the organizer do something with regard to having vegetarian food at the next barbecue. In her opening sentence, Stefanie claims an implicit authority by speaking on behalf of both the reader and the speakers (the children in our class).

In her letter, Stefanie is adamant, using the phrase *have to* with regard to making available vegetarian hot dogs and hamburgers. Earlier in the day, P.J. and Melanie also talked to Stefanie about using *have to* as a way of telling someone you are serious. They said that saying "please" would be polite, but that it probably would not work in this situation. The word *please*, they said, would imply that we are asking if we can have vegetarian food at the next barbecue rather than taking a stand on the issue. According to Stefanie, "Mostly please is good to use but not this time."

Anthony had contributed to the letter writing by saying, "My daddy knows where to buy vegetarian food." Stefanie felt that letting the chair know where to buy the food was a good idea because it was a way of helping solve the problem and further demonstrating how serious we really were about dealing with this issue and that we do know what we are talking about. Also, there is a sense of immediacy and an expectation for action associated with having written, "You can ask Anthony's daddy where to buy vegetarian food" rather than "Anthony's daddy knows where to buy vegetarian food."

Once the letter was written, Stefanie and a friend deposited it in the interschool mailbox. Then it was time to wait for a response. My students became increasingly frustrated with waiting. I used this waiting time as an opportunity to talk to the group about follow-up letters and sending multiple letters as two ways of showing the seriousness of your intent. I also talked to them about rereading our original letter to find better ways with words to get our message across. In a sense I wanted my students to "ache with caring" (Fox, 1993, p. 3) over their writing in order for their letter to do the work they had wanted: to send a clear message regarding the need to have vegetarian food at our school barbecue. Stefanie decided that a follow-up letter was in order. Two weeks after sending the original letter, she had a discussion about follow-up letters with P.J., Melanie, and Anthony and then shared, with the whole group during meeting time, her intent to write a second letter. In this letter she wrote,

> Dear Mr. Andrews,
> Vegetarians need food too. They don't eat meat so they can't eat at the barbecue. Because they don't eat hamburgers because they are vegetarian.
>
> Please have food for vegetarians at the next barbecue.
>
> Stefanie

P.S. Please write me back. What happened
to the letter I gave you from before?

In the second letter, Stefanie took an explicative approach by
explaining what vegetarians can't eat by stating they don't eat meat,
they can't eat hamburgers, and they can't eat at the barbecue. In a
sense, she used this approach as a rationale for the position she was
taking in support of vegetarians. This time she opted to return to
the use of *please* to see if "Maybe the chair might understand better
and want to listen to us more." She had set up "a sense of certainty
and authority, a polite but insistent tone" (Comber & Kamler, 1997,
p. 47). Stefanie again made clear the seriousness of her issue and
clarified the intent of her original letter by asking the chair to write
back. She also made clear that this was not the first time that she
had attempted to bring this issue to administrative attention. This
time, however, she did receive a response. The chair of the school
barbecue committee invited Stefanie to the office to talk about her
concerns. She wrote,

> MMM   Veggie Food,
> Next BBQ we'll have food
> for vegetarians for sure.
> Do you have any helpful
> suggestions?! Come to my
> office soon to discuss.
> Thank you

Extending Our Literacies

Encouraged, the children decided to find out more about vegetarians in order to prepare for the meeting. They turned for help to
our school librarian. To their surprise, they were told that there were
no books about vegetarians in our library. Another letter was written, this time to the school librarian. Stefanie and her friends were
learning how to make use of the critical literacies they were learning, extending these to another situation. In this letter she wrote,

> Dear Mr. Librarian,
> Libraries are for kids and all people.

Vegetarians are people but there's no books
about them in the library. There should be
books about all people in the library.

She began her letter by stating what she knew about libraries:
"Libraries are for kids and all people." She then used the word "people" to link each of her sentences; libraries are for people, vegetarians are people, there should be books for all people. When I spoke
with her about this, she referred to the strategy as a "pattern" like in
Quick as a Cricket and *Brown Bear, Brown Bear*, two picture books
that make use of patterned text.

As the children had expected, the librarian was very supportive of their concern and even asked Anthony if he knew of any
good books that we should have in the library, as well as telling the
children that he would make sure to order some books on being a
vegetarian.

Further Extensions of the Vegetarian Issue

During class meeting one day, Melissa made the comment that
if at our school we "forgot about people like vegetarians, maybe
other schools did too." Considering what she could do to find out if
her hypothesis was true, and encouraged by the response Stefanie
received for her letters, Melissa decided to compose her own letter
to send to other elementary schools in our district. She wrote,

Dear Principal,
We want to check that the
vegetarians have food at the next
barbecue in your school, if you have one.
Our friend couldn't eat at our barbecue because
he is a vegetarian and that wasn't fair. Now we
want to take care that all the kids can eat at the
barbecue even the vegetarians.

In her opening sentence, she was explicit about the aim of the
letter, which was to find out whether there were vegetarians at the
school, whether the school had an annual barbecue, and if so, was vegetarian food made available? She put herself in a position of authority
when stating, "Our friend couldn't eat at our barbecue because he is a

vegetarian and that wasn't fair." By adding this sentence, she made it clear that she was speaking from a position of experience. She closed her letter by restating her concern as an issue of equity.

Melissa wanted to make sure she received a response so I discussed various options with her and looked at notes and letters that had previously been sent home where parents were asked to respond in some way. She predicted the notes with the tear-away sections would be most effective. She also suspected that if whoever answers the survey has to do too much work, he or she might not respond. She told me that she knew that might happen because her mom says, "I don't have time for all this writing" when filling out various forms for school. Mainly wanting to find out where other schools were in terms of having food available for vegetarians at their school events, Melissa decided she wanted her survey "to be just yes and no questions to check off." I asked her what information would be most useful to her, at which time we worked on the questions included in her survey (see Fig. 4.1).

We sent out over two dozen surveys and received three responses. Of the three responses, there was consensus that none of the three schools had thought about vegetarians being left out of school events when vegetarian food was not made available. Each also ticked off the box saying that they would make sure that they have vegetarian food at future events.

The low response did not discourage the children. Their take was that they tried something new that probably was unexpected coming from such young children and in spite of this, some

---

ABOUT VEGETARIANS SURVEY

What is the name of your school? _____

Do you have a school barbecue?   YES☐   NO☐

                                                                 YES☐   NO☐

Do you think it is fair not to have food for vegetarians? YES☐   NO☐

Are you going to have vegetarian food if you have   YES☐   NO☐
Vegetarians?

FIG. 4.1.   Melissa's Vegetarian Survey.

people responded. They said that maybe next time they'd get a better response. They were excited to have received the responses they did and to see that the survey had worked even if only for a limited extent. Together, we talked about the possible reasons behind the low response. I shared my thoughts with them and they shared theirs with me. I think Melanie's comment was most enlightening. She said, "Caring about vegetarians is not important to some people because they don't know any vegetarians. We have to just keep on helping people to get to care about people even if they don't know them." In a way, they were learning a different way of being and participating in the world.

In order to represent the vegetarian issue on our audit trail, we decided to post a copy of the first letter that had been written, as well as the book cover (Fig. 4.2) for *Where the Forest Meets the Sea.* The letter reminds us of the action we took and the book cover reminds us of the connection between earlier studies regarding environmental issues and the vegetarian issue.

FIG. 4.2. Artifact Representing the Vegetarian Issue on Our Audit Trail.

Reflective Summary

The letter-writing campaign in support of vegetarians certainly brought to the fore questions regarding who else may be marginalized in some way at school. How might others be marginalized or "othered" because space is not provided for them? In our case, it was not until 4-year-old Anthony made his comment regarding not eating at the school barbecue and his peers took social action that the marginalization of vegetarians was brought to our awareness. There is a high probability that if the children and I had not had previous conversations regarding equity in the classroom, Anthony's issue, which turned out to be a whole-class issue and then a school issue, would not have been noticed. To me, this is a clear indication that in order to be critical, one must lead a critically literate life. I believe that it was framing our living, as a class, through critical literacy that allowed us to recognize the unfair treatment of vegetarians at our school. Taking this up as a topic for study in our curriculum led to changing the status of vegetarians in our school.

Close to the end of the school year, there were three social events held at our school for various reasons and different groups of people. One was the Junior Kindergarten and Senior Kindergarten Family Picnic, another the Staff End-of-Year Party, and the third a birthday party for a staff member. In all three cases, vegetarian options were made available. In 12 years as a teacher with this particular school board, the option for vegetarian food was never before made available at the schools where I taught.

The letter writing engaged in by Stefanie and Melissa represents those instances when action begins locally and then is raised on a broader scale. It also demonstrates what happens when young children begin to unpack the relationship between language and power by engaging in some form of discourse analysis. Through their letter writing, they were able to position themselves differently as child writers, and on behalf of their peers, as well as for the vegetarians at our school and community.

Critical Reflections and Pedagogical Questions

Peter Johnston (2004) reminds us "the intellectual life is social, it is also relational and emotional" (p. 2). He suggests that our students' discursive histories are the stuff that makes it possible for them to say what they say. Further, he notes, "teachers play a critical role in arranging the discursive histories from which [they] speak" (p. 3). As such, the words teachers choose and the discourses they make available help mediate children's activity and experience and, at the same time, help them make sense of learning, literacy, and themselves.

The vegetarian story is a good example of what happens when children have opportunities to play with and understand the effects of their word choices. The ways in which children can do this depends in part on the kinds of spaces we have created in our classrooms for them to "play their way into literacies" (Wohlwend, 2011, p. 1) and try on different words that allow them to take up the best positions possible with respect to the work at hand and "with respect to others in their social environment" (Johnston, 2004, p. 23).

What might this mean for you in your setting? How might you offer more powerful discursive practices that create opportunities for the children with whom you work to participate differently in the world so that they can be productive citizens who contribute to changing inequitable ways of being?

So far, I have shared instances of questioning and analyzing social texts with my students that led to taking social action. In the next chapter, I outline how my students and I used a social text to reread a more traditional school text.

5

Save the Beluga

Setting the Scene

Lily arrived at school one day excited to talk about a news report she had seen on television the night before. The report was about the beluga in the St. Lawrence River in southeastern Canada, and the pollution that was endangering their lives. The pollution was caused by chemical waste dumped into the water by a manufacturing company on the shore of the river. Lily learned that the beluga in the St. Lawrence were absorbing toxic chemical waste into their bodies and that as a result, they were in danger of becoming extinct from that area. In this chapter, I describe the learning and social action that unfolded as my students and I used this media text to reread a picture book.

Save the Beluga

"Baby Beluga," performed by the children's entertainer Raffi (1992), was a song that the children loved to sing. It was about a beluga calf. Given our new knowledge about what was happening to the whales in the St. Lawrence River, I decided to revisit, with my students, the picture book version of the song (Fig. 5.1) to see whether they would read the book differently given what they had just learned about the beluga in the St. Lawrence. In doing so, we compared how the texts, the news report, and the song/picture book represent the beluga. (For the remainder of this chapter, I refer to the song/picture book as "the book" or "the song" when referring to the text.)

In order to explore how texts build up particular portrayals of subject matter, we engaged in text analysis by creating word lists to describe how the beluga were portrayed in the book and the news report. First, we generated a list of words that described the whales in the news report and came up with the following list:

- In danger
- Not safe
- Needs help
- Sick
- Dying
- No power
- Hurt
- Hungry
- Scared

I then read the book out loud, and then we created a second list of words to describe how the whales were portrayed in the book. Our list included the following words:

- Free
- Happy
- Snug
- Safe
- Fun life
- On the go
- Comfortable
- Splashing around for fun

We studied both sets of words to consider how the whales were presented in each text. In essence, what I was trying to do here was to get at the dominant themes and discourses of each text. This activity was a good way to help my students understand how texts are constructed.

One of the children asked, "So what is real? Which one is real?" Another child noticed, "The words in one is like the opposite of the

FIG. 5.1. *Baby Beluga* Picture Book.

other words." We discovered that the texts offered binary oppositions or opposite portrayals of life for the beluga; humane and happy
versus inhumane and in danger of extinction. For me, this brought
the realization that "for at least some of the children the boundar-
ies between life in books and life as they understand it are blurred"
(O'Brien, 1998, p. 10). In response, I talked to them about how different texts offer different perspectives of the world and the way the
world works. We also talked about how important it is to think about
other ways that a text could be written or presented and how the
words chosen by the authors of the text shape the way we think about
an issue or topic. The children talked about how they liked singing
the song but that the song "doesn't give us a good idea of what is
happening with the whales in the [St. Lawrence] river." "Raffi didn't
say anything about the whales being in danger," they continued. In
response, we wrote our own version of the song (Fig. 5.2) to see
if we could come up with a more accurate representation of the
whales.

**Save the Beluga Song
By the J.K.s**

Baby Beluga in the deep blue sea
please help us so we can be.
The garbage in the water
doesn't let us be free.
Please save us from this pollution.

Baby Beluga, Baby Beluga.
Is the water safe?
Is the water clean?
For us to live in?

Baby Beluga in the deep blue sea
please help us so we can be.
The garbage in the water
doesn't let us be free.
Please save us from this pollution.

Please save us from this pollution.

FIG. 5.2.   Revised "Baby Beluga" Song.

First, I wrote the song lyrics from the picture book on a large sheet of poster paper and propped it up on our easel. We read the text together and then I asked the children to think about who was doing the talking in the song. "Raffi is talking," was their immediate reply. The discussion continued.

Teacher:	What I want you to do now is to think about the words carefully and think about who Raffi was talking to.
Tiffany:	He's talking to us right? About Baby Beluga?
Gregory:	That's the audience, like think about the audience!
Ali:	Ya, remember our letters. Who are you writing for? Remember that question? Mrs. Vasquez asked us that.
Teacher:	We did talk about that a while ago, that writers write for an audience. One audience is our class.

We had talked about purposes and functions of writing as we engaged in learning about vegetarians and about taking social action to be included in the French Café (see Chapter 3). We had also talked about writing as a powerful form of language use in society. In the last exchange, the children show what it means to extend what they learned in one context to another. Our discussion continued.

> Teacher: Let's look at the words more carefully and then think about who Raffi is talking to within the song. We already know that we are one audience.
> Lee: I think he might be talking to Baby Beluga.
> Teacher: How do you know? What are some clues?
> Melissa: (singing) Baby Beluga in the deep blue sea (humming without words) (in a loud voice) YOU swim so free!
> P.J.: Or "Is your mama home with you?"
> Teacher: Well let's see if we can pick out all the phrases that are like the ones Melissa and P.J. noticed.

As the children identified similar phrases, I underlined them on the chart paper that had the song lyrics. We found that the words *you* and *your* were used 11 times in the song. We then talked about the effect that using phrases such as "you swim so free" or "you dive and splash all day" have on the reader, specifically on us as readers. To do this, I asked the children to read the text with me once more, this time replacing *you* with *I* (e.g., "I swim so free" or "I dive and splash all day"). We experimented further by replacing *you* with *we*. The children decided that they liked the effect of using *we* because it refers to "more than just one" beluga "like in the St. Lawrence." They also said that kids like animals talking and that "young kids would really like the song if the beluga or the beluga family was doing the talking instead of Raffi talking to Baby Beluga." We kept all of this in mind as we began crafting our version of the beluga song.

We also talked about how two different texts presented the same topic (the life of the beluga) and discussed what each text tried to do to us as readers. For example, we discussed how the book tried to draw us in by using patterned and predictable words and phrases about the beluga, while the news report worked to bring some awareness regarding the endangerment of the whales, causing us to want to get involved with saving them by taking some form of action.

Doing this kind of analysis led to talking about other ways of writing about the beluga that helped us to craft our revised version of the song. Our version took into account our new knowledge about the whales in the St. Lawrence. Reconstructing the beluga song was one way to interrupt the dominant reading of the book and in doing so, construct different meanings. Working on revising the song lyrics included not only becoming more aware of the current state of the belugas in the St. Lawrence but considering the role that language plays to shape our thinking.

I believe the work we did with analyzing the different texts is a good demonstration of what happens when readers engage in multiple readings of varied text such as news articles, graphics in cover designs, and song lyrics.

Baby Beluga Take Two: Our Version

To begin crafting our version of the song, I asked the children what they thought the theme of the song should be and what message we wanted to convey. We decided that most important was to bring awareness to the plight of the beluga. Following this, we referred to our lists and further brainstormed words including *safe* and *clean*, and phrases such as "save us from pollution" and "help us live" for possible inclusion. As we chose the words and phrases to include in our song, we engaged in various discussions. For example, there was a discussion over whether "please save us from this pollution" more effectively conveys the plight of the beluga than "you will be saved from this pollution" or "we will save you from this pollution." We talked about how the second and third choices seemed to focus more on who is helping to save the beluga instead of the endangerment of the beluga. We finished our song after several of these discussions. After this, a group of children began rehearsing singing the song, which they performed for other classes as a way of bringing awareness to the plight of the beluga.

Grounding Our Work in Social Intent with Real-World Effects

Producing an alternative rewriting or reconstruction (Luke, Comber, & O'Brien, 1996) of the beluga song was one way that we took an active citizenry role. Another way was by raising money for an animal activist fund (Fig. 5.3). Therefore, our analysis was not limited to deconstructing text but led to the reconstruction of a new text where the reconstruction of text was grounded in social intent and real world effects. For example, while searching the World Wide Web for information on whales with her mom at home, one of the girls found the World Wildlife Fund of Canada (WWF Canada) site. She learned that WWF Canada had been doing research to find ways of sustaining the population in the St. Lawrence. She also learned that this organization accepts donations to support their efforts. In fact, the Web page includes a number of tips for taking action, from holding bake sales to writing letters. At one of our class meetings, some of the children suggested that we send the money from our classroom store to WWF Canada.

The children ran our classroom store. Basically, they would repackage cereal into small bags. These were made available for children who either forgot their snack or wanted to have cereal for snack. Children could take a bag of cereal and contribute at least 10¢ to our store fund. It was the money that had been accumulating in this fund that we decided to contribute to the WWF of Canada. As a reminder of this action, we decided to rename our store the "Save the Beluga Store"

FIG. 5.3.   Our Save the Belugas Store.

FIG. 5.4.   Artifacts Representing the Beluga Issue on Our Audit Trail.

The artifacts in Fig. 5.4 represent the work that we did to analyze different portrayals of whales in various texts. We decided to post a book cover and a drawing. The book cover was posted to remind us of "Baby," one of the texts we unpacked. The drawing was included to remind us of the action that we took to raise money for the WWF.

Further Opportunities for Analyzing the Book

Further analysis that we could have done includes looking for other books and news articles about belugas to analyze what the dominant themes, patterns, and discourses were and whether these were ideologically slanted. In other words, we could have explored whose interests are served by different portrayals of subject matter. Doing this would have further built my students' analytic skills for examining how language works to refract, distort, and position (Luke et al., 1996).

Analyzing the Beluga Incident

The text is a common kind of text read in preschool and early primary classrooms. It is the kind of book deemed to support early readers through the repetition and patterning of words and phrases. However, even a seemingly innocent text can be used alternatively in the classroom when paired with other texts that allow the reader to reinterpret it by asking different questions, such as how it has been constructed and how it might be written in a different way. The experiences we engaged in created space for my students to examine the narrowness of representations in certain texts. If we had not considered the media segment regarding the beluga in the St. Lawrence River, the book *Baby Beluga* might have remained unopposed as the key shaper of the children's perceptions of whales.

The action to support the cause of the whales was not just about accumulating knowledge to discover more about a particular topic or to become better educated about environmental issues. The experience involved what Comber (2001) referred to as mobilizing student knowledge with social intent and real world effects. That is, using what children know, the experiences they bring as "cultural capital" (Bourdieu, 1991) to do life work. Deconstructing the book text and the everyday media text provided a space to explore the social construction of truth and reality.

In the next chapter, I show how my students and I worked with other kinds of everyday texts to take up issues such as consumerism and gender.

Critical Reflections and Pedagogical Questions

For me, an important element of imagining spaces for critical literacies is to take a look back and critically reflect on and deconstruct the work that we do in the same way that we would any other text. I believe doing this helps us to better understand the real world effects of the work that we do. Subsequently, this kind of self-critical analysis helps us to make more informed decisions regarding what to do and where to go next with our teaching.

A step back from the beluga study for instance gives me a chance to consider what more we could have done to push our learning. Through the years, I have received many pieces of correspondence from readers of the first edition of this text. Often, readers share with me what they are doing in their classrooms to create spaces for critical literacies. What I have noticed with stories shared about work with endangered species is that there seems to be particular animals that are central to this work. Most of these animals can be considered cute, such as pandas and belugas. Earlier in this chapter you read about my students sending proceeds from our classroom store to the WWF of Canada. They do good work and I believe they ought to be supported. At the same time however, organizations like WWF are in part responsible for the focus on cute endangered animals. After all, it is more likely that a patron would support the cause of a cute animal rather than an ugly one.

Take the tarsier for instance (Fig. 5.5). This little creature is not only endangered; it is on the critically endangered animal list. The Tasmanian devil (Fig. 5.6) is another animal in danger of extinction. In fact, according to the website Zooborns, the species is in danger of disappearing in the next 20 years. Further, from the website, I learned that the wild populations of devils in Tasmania already have plummeted in some areas by 85%.

In 14 years teaching preschool and elementary school not once did I hear about tarsiers. Nor did I ever hear of anyone, myself included, who was studying Tasmanian devils with their students. Why is that? What does this tell us about what we value and privilege

FIG. 5.5. Tarsier.

in society? What can we do to change this perspective on endangered not so cuddly species?

One activity is to have a close look at the WWF website specifically exploring the adoption pages. As of this writing, the Canadian Wildlife Fund has the following animals available for symbolic adoption: snowy owl, Kermode bear, gorilla, orca, river otter, polar bear, giant panda, emperor penguin, jaguar, lynx, grey wolf, orangutan, tiger, walrus, grizzly bear, Arctic fox, black-footed ferret, blue shark and meerkat. You can view the adorable stuffed animals for adopting at wwfstore.donorportal.ca/c-41-all-adoptions.aspx. The US WWF site at gifts.worldwildlife.org/gift-center/gifts/Species-Adoptions.aspx includes many more animals than the Canadian site, including the tarsier and the Tasmanian devil. Interestingly enough, however, on the US site, there is a Build-Your-Own-Bucket page (gifts.worldwildlife.org/gift-center/gifts/Buckets/Build-Your-Own-Bucket.aspx).

FIG. 5.6. Tasmanian Devil.

Here you can symbolically adopt a bucket of 3 to 4 animals. Unfortunately, the tarsier and the Tasmanian devil did not make it on the Build-Your-Own-Bucket page. Why might that be? Who is advantaged by this move to make available particularly cute stuffed animals rather than those that are less than cuddly? What purpose does this serve? Who is disadvantaged by this? These are just a few questions to consider if you were to explore this topic of study with your students.

Following is a beginning resource list that might inform work that you do regarding critically endangered species if this topic is of interest to your students.

Resources on Critically Endangered Species

"Smiling" Tarsier Among New Most Endangered Species
http://news.nationalgeographic.com/news/2011/06/pictures/
110622-iucn-red-list-critically-endangered-species-animals/

Species Directory
http://worldwildlife.org/species/directory?sort=extinction_
status&direction=desc

Tarsier.org
http://www.tarsier.org/about_tarsiers.html

Tasmanian Devil
http://animals.nationalgeographic.com/animals/mammals/
tasmanian-devil/

The Northern Sportive Lemur
http://www.allaboutwildlife.com/the-northern-sportive-lemur

The Philippine Tarsier Foundation
http://www.tarsierfoundation.org/the-philippine-tarsier

The 100 Most Threatened Species
http://www.zsl.org/conservation/news/the-100-most-threat
ened-species,997,NS.html

6

We Know How McDonald's Thinks

Setting the Scene

The instances of learning that I describe in this chapter focus on interrogating and analyzing discourses that are associated with McDonald's Happy Meals™. The work that we did with the Happy Meal was initiated when Ali, one of the girls in the class, started a conversation with a small group of children about Happy Meal toys. By this time in the school year (spring 1997), my students already had many opportunities to analyze different school and everyday texts. Therefore, they had built up quite a repertoire of critical literacies and were comfortable interrogating McDonald's Happy Meals as text.

The McDonald's Happy Meal as Text

In the following conversation, Ali introduced the Happy Meal toy for discussion because this was a topic that interested her. What resulted was a series of activities, engagements, and discussions exploring how Happy Meals work, including how McDonald's uses

147

toys as a way of maintaining child consumers and the gendered way they went about doing this.

1 Ali:	At McDonald's they have different toys.
2 Stefanie:	Yah. Like now there's Beanie Babies™. It's a goldfish I think.
3 Ali:	Well, before it was different. Like there were little Barbie™ and Hot Wheels™.
4 Michael:	Yah, but the person actually said you're a boy so I'll put a Hot Wheel in your Happy Meal. Except I already had that car so I wanted a Barbie for my sister.
5 Alyssa:	Well I'm a girl but I got a Hot Wheel.
6 Michael:	I guess so. Sometimes stuff that's girls', boys like and stuff that's boys' girls like and . . .
7 Alyssa:	And if you tell the McDonald's people what you want then you can have the toy you want.

In this opening discussion, the children began to raise questions about McDonald's take on what toys girls like and what toys boys like. In doing so, they were interpreting their experiences within the McDonald's gendered discourse and problematizing that discourse. This is seen when Michael stated, "Yah, but the person actually said you're a boy so I'll put a Hot Wheel in your Happy Meal. Except I already had that car so I wanted a Barbie for my sister" (line 4). When he later agrees with Alyssa and adds that "Sometimes stuff that's girls', boys like and stuff that's boys' girls like," (line 6) he elaborates on his initial comment to make the point that some boys may want a doll and some girls may want a toy car and that is okay.

As the children interpreted their experiences, they also shared ways they had acted differently within McDonald's gender bias discourse, as demonstrated when Alyssa said "Well, I'm a girl and I got a Hot Wheel" (line 5) and then explained how she did this by saying, "If you tell the McDonald's people what you want then you can have what you want" (line 7). With this statement, she implicitly shared with the other children how she had disrupted the gendered discourse by stating what she wanted. In a subsequent conversation, she explained that "If you don't tell people what you want then boys will get Hot Wheels and girls will get Barbies." This is quite sophisticated thinking that underlies one way in which problematic ways of being and ways of thinking are normalized and/or naturalized. If we do not speak up or "tell people what we want," then dominant problematic discourses will prevail and "boys will get Hot Wheels and girls will get Barbies."

We Know How McDonald's Thinks: The Discussion Continues

As the discussion continued, the children began to unpack "how McDonald's thinks"; what their agenda was for changing the Happy Meal toys on an ongoing basis.

8 Curtis:	They always change the toys.
9 Teacher:	Why do you think they do that?
10 Ali:	Well, maybe it's because they know we like toys.
11 Teacher:	Do you mean children like toys or adults or both?
12 Ali:	I think both but mostly kids that's why there's toys in Happy Meals.
13 Tiffany:	Yah that's why.
14 Andrew:	Well, if they didn't change the toys I wouldn't go.
15 Michael:	Me either.
16 Andrew:	Actually that tells me McDonald's knows how we think! But now. Now, we know how they think. Aha!

Curtis' statement "They always change the toys" (line 8) pushed the discussion in a different direction that focused on one of the ways McDonald's maintains child consumers. They hypothesized that McDonald's included toys in the Happy Meals because they know that children like toys. In other words, pairing a toy with a meal makes the whole eating experience more pleasurable, which translates to becoming hooked as a satisfied customer. Further, they hypothesized that changing the toys is the strategy used to make sure children come back for more, thereby promoting collecting behavior. According to Andrew, "If they didn't change the toys I wouldn't go" (line 14). With this, he surmised, "McDonald's knows how we [children] think" (line 16). In other words, McDonald's knows that if they do not use strategies such as including new toys in the Happy Meals, children like Andrew would not keep returning. Making this strategy visible led Andrew to conclude that McDonald's may know how we think but "Now, we know how they think. Aha!" (line 16). Recognizing this statement as an opportunity to explore what it means to be an informed consumer led me to dig deeper at what the children thought McDonald's knew about kids.

17 Teacher:	What do you think it is that they know about kids and how kids think?
18 Andrew:	One thing they know is . . .
19 Melanie:	Well, one thing is that no new toys, no kids!
20 Curtis:	Yah. 'Cause lots of kids go for the collectibles. There's always collectibles.
21 Teacher:	Tell us more about that.
22 Curtis:	Collectibles, you collect. Like, this week you get a Goldfish Beanie and next week you get a plat. . . a plat . . .
23 Ali:	A platypus.
24 Alyssa:	A platypus. So if you keep going back you can have the whole collection.

Reflecting on **How McDonald's Thinks**

As the children engaged in talk about collections and being a collector, they simultaneously uncovered the ideological construction of the Happy Meal, which is why Happy Meals come with toys. The conclusions they came up with, that kids "go for the collectibles" (line 20), was consistent with those described in a *USA Today* article about a recent McDonald's marketing campaign, the McFurby™. This was a promotional campaign that explicitly advertised the desirability of collecting dozens of different McFurbys: small plastic versions of the talking Furby™ produced by Hasbro. The article described McDonald's development of the McFurby promotion and the role that children play in the success of food sales as a direct result of such promotions (Horovitz, 1999).

The report stated that McDonald's knows it has a delicate sales job to convince its most vital customers—kids. The report claimed that children influence almost two thirds of the $110 billion that Americans spend annually on fast food. According to the report, "A super-hot toy promotion can rocket overall food sales 6% to 9% during its run" and "Kids will drag their parents to McDonald's kicking and screaming to get their mitts on Furby Happy Meals." One of the report's conclusions was that "McDonald's kids promotions have become habit forming." This is also consistent with my students' analysis as exemplified when Alyssa commented, "If you keep going back you can have the whole collection" (line 24) and when

Andrew stated that if McDonald's didn't keep changing the toys, kids wouldn't keep coming (line 14).

The children also talked about having to go back to gather each of the collectible items in a series. An example of this took place when Curtis explained that collectibles mean that you collect, "like, this week you get a goldfish [Beanie Baby] and next week you get a platypus [Beanie Baby]" (line 22). According to Alyssa, the point is to keep going back until you have the whole collection (line 24). One of the goals for going to McDonald's, then, is to complete each of the collections. These collections vary in size from eight Barbies in the year 2000 promotion to over two-dozen McFurbys in the 1997 Furby promotion. Remember, each Happy Meal comes with one toy only, although extra toys could be purchased at an extra cost. However, with most promotions, the different toys in a collection are released at different times, which means multiple trips back to the restaurant. According to the *USA Today* article (1999), "Collectibility is what Happy Meals is about." In a column written by columnist Bruce Horovitz (1999) in the same edition of *USA Today*, he wrote, "The world changed in 1979 when McDonald's introduced its first national Happy Meal with plastic figurines from Star Trek." Further, he stated, "Licensing (of rights to toys representing films such as *Star Trek*) is the fast food industry's mantra. . . . Entire staffs of marketing gurus are constantly on the lookout for the next hot kids toy, tune flick or TV shows." In their own way, the children were able to recognize what is obviously a complex corporate strategy. One thing that we could have looked into more carefully was exploring McDonald's partnerships with other corporations to consider how the Happy Meal frenzy is not only about selling McDonald's food but advertising and merchandising for other film and toy companies with whom they have formed equally profitable relationships.

Who Can Have Collectibles?

In the following exchange, the children engage in a discussion about fairness and access to collectible items, addressing the question of who can and cannot be a collector.

25 Andrew: When you have the whole collection, except not everyone can get the whole collection. You know my neighbor, well, they have seven kids in their family. That's a lot of kids.

26 Lily: That's a lot of Happy Meals.

27 Andrew: And a lot of Big Macs™ if the mom or the dad eats.
28 Ali: Yah or the nanas [grandmothers].
29 Andrew: Yah so what I wanted to say is they don't get to
                   go all the time so they can't collect ALL of them.
30 Gregory: It's really not fair.
31 Michael: See, there's something else we can know about
                   McDonald's. It's not fair that everybody can't
                   have the collectibles.

Reflecting on the Conversation

In that exchange (lines 25–31), the children raised issues of fairness regarding who has and does not have access to Happy Meal collectibles. Andrew set the issue in context by talking about what he knew of his neighbors who have "seven kids in their family" (line 25). Further into the conversation, he returned to this issue, clarifying what it was he meant by bringing forward his neighbors' situation, saying, "They don't get to go all the time so they can't collect ALL of them" (line 29). He clarified the issue as being one of collectibility and the subsequent unfair or inequitable access that children have to collectibles. In our school, children formed clubs during recess, while in the schoolyard, as a way to show their latest collectible acquisitions. So on any given recess period, children could be seen gathered in groups based on these informal clubs. Andrew worried about what this meant for his neighbors when they were in the schoolyard. Would they be marginalized if left out of such activities?

In rare cases, a child could become a member of a club without having to display his or her wares as long as the child was able to present a good deal of knowledge about the item being collected. Being able to talk knowingly about collectibles, therefore, was a discourse that brought children a good deal of cultural capital (Bourdieu, 1991) in the schoolyard. The downside of this is that it is, of course, difficult to gain a good deal of knowledge about the collectible items without having access to them.

Further Analysis of the Happy Meal

As the conversation continued, the children began to name the ways in which McDonald's constructed them as consumers through the use of clever promotional strategies.

32 Andrew:	Yea and then they change them all the time. (Referring to the Happy Meal toys)
33 Teacher:	Why do you think they do that?
34 Alyssa:	Well, kids won't go if they don't.
35 Gregory:	We said that before. Remember. We know how McDonald's thinks. They think if they don't put toys in the food pack that kids won't want to eat their food.
36 Curtis:	That's like tricking kids because they trick them to buy food by pretending they give them toys.
37 Andrew:	My dad said, "The price of the toy is in the bag."
38 Michael:	What?
39 Teacher:	Did your dad mean that the price of the toy is included as part of the whole Happy Meal package?
40 Andrew:	That's what I said. Yea that's what I mean. You got it.

Reflecting on the Conversation

In this particular portion of our conversation, the children made it clear that they were not naive to why McDonald's uses different sets of toys in their promotions. Further, they talked about McDonald's manipulation of child consumers in the way they present the promotional toys as included "free" in Happy Meals. The children talked about how McDonald's "pretends to give" the toys away (line 36). A conversation regarding this issue had obviously come up in Andrew's home as indicated by his statement, "My dad said, it's in the bag" (line 37). This statement made it clear that to some extent, Andrew had an understanding of how consumers are charged with hidden costs. So the apparently free toys were not free after all.

In response to Andrew's comment and to consider McDonald's notion of "free" toys and what "free" really costs, we created a web of what makes up a Happy Meal (Fig. 6.1). The original web (Fig. 6.2) consists of the parts of the Happy Meal that are immediately visible to the consumer, such as a hamburger, toy, and french fries. After this initial webbing, I asked the children to think about each item in the Happy Meal and then brainstorm all of the things that are part of each of those items (Fig. 6.3). We then went back to our web a third

FIG. 6.1. Happy Meal Web.

time and talked about all the things they could think of that are part of each of the items listed during our second webbing activity (see Fig. 6.1). To differentiate each of the lists, I used a different color marker.

Andrew summarized what this webbing activity made visible for us when he said, "For something that's free there's lots of people who sell things and get money." Through our analysis of the Happy Meal, the children realized that many people have investments in children as consumers.

FIG. 6.2. The First Round of Webbing: What Is in a Happy Meal?

FIG. 6.3. A Second Round of Webbing.

Final Thoughts on the Happy Meal Discussions in the Classroom

The McDonald's issue is somewhat more complicated to talk about than the issues dealt with in previous chapters because of the various subtexts that were generated, such as the susceptibility of child consumers and gender construction through the distribution of Happy Meal toys. What the subtexts have in common, however, is that each questions the taken-for-granted normality to consider how things could be different (Comber, 1999). This happens through using what children know, their experience with McDonald's as a starting point for analysis, and then unpacking texts such as the Happy Meal. Informed by practices demonstrated in the literature on critical literacy (Kamler, 1994; O'Brien, 1998) disrupting taken-for-granted normality (Comber, 1999) happened as we engaged with questions like, What kinds of things do you learn from analyzing what makes up a Happy Meal? Or, What do the toys in the Happy Meals tell you about being a girl or being a boy? In this way, the children are able to begin to make visible new ways of being and acting that involve resisting dominant practices such as giving girls Barbies and giving boys Hot Wheels.

Social Action Outside the Classroom

"Although children are not direct income earners, they are in charge of more (pocket) money than in the past, and they also exert significant power over parental purchase choices" (Luke, 1997, p. 21). Shortly after we engaged in our McDonald's conversation, before we could send home a newsletter about it, the mother of one of my students came up to me and asked if we had talked about McDonald's in our classroom. Apparently, since Melanie was about 2 years old, she and her parents had had a routine whereby every Sunday they would go to McDonald's after church.

As our work with the Happy Meal as text was wrapping up, McDonald's was receiving a lot of publicity from the famous McLibel trial whereby McDonald's sued a couple of activists for libel regarding a pamphlet they had distributed revealing the ways in which the food giant engaged in such practices as animal cruelty, waste production, and rain forest depletion (Klein, 2001). As a direct result of the work we had done regarding McDonald's in our classroom and what she had heard on the news about the McLibel trial, Melanie decided that she no longer wanted to support McDonald's as a consumer. In essence, she decided to boycott McDonald's. In response, her mother had suggested going to another local fast-food burger restaurant. According to her mother, Melanie quickly pointed out that the other restaurant was no better because she felt that they manipulated child consumers by changing or adding equipment to their Playland on an ongoing basis as well as by giving out toys as a way to keep young customers buying their products in the same way McDonald's did.

The reason I like this story is because it shows the kinds of literacies that are constructed through the critical literacy practices in our classroom and, most importantly, how these literacies extend into the lives of the children outside of school. As Melanie grew as a literate learner in our classroom, she also learned to read the world and versions of the possible roles she could take in the world (O'Brien, 1998). She has begun to understand how the world as text works on her and what she can do to respond to that text. She was capable of sharing her ideas and influencing others.

While engaged with McDonald's as text, multilayered conversations were constructed; different children involved themselves with different activities and actions in response to the text.

As you can see, the issues we dealt with were very generative. We were never short of ideas for projects or issues and topics to research. There was always more for yet another day. The following section demonstrates ways that we used what we discovered through our previous conversations and analysis to reimagine ways of repackaging McDonald's toys.

Designing a Toy Container

While we were analyzing the McDonald's Happy Meal, a small group of children began looking closely at the plastic bag used to package some of the toys. They started by asking me to read out loud the text on the bag. They were particularly interested in the warning label, which read:

WARNING: TO AVOID DANGER OF SUFFOCATION, KEEP BAG AWAY FROM BABIES AND CHILDREN. DISPOSE OF THIS BAG IMMEDIATELY.
(© 1999 McDonald's Corporation)

My students argued that if the bag was so hazardous, then why were they used to package the toys inasmuch as children purchase the toys. Gregory suggested that the packaging really should be changed. In response, a group of four students designed their own toy containers, which they felt were safer for children.

One of the designs was a small box to hold the promotional toy. Another suggestion involved recycling McDonald's wrappers. Someone else came up with a bag similar to party favor bags. Gregory was one of the children who designed a box. Once having thought about how to design his box, he hand-delivered his proposal (Fig. 6.4) to the McDonald's branch close to his home. At the end of the school year, we had not heard back from McDonald's. However, Gregory did say that if he didn't hear back soon that he would see if he could "do it on the Internet." Looking closely at his letter, it is interesting to note that, similar to the letters written by his classmates to deal with the vegetarian issue, Gregory's letter also demonstrated the assertion of identity through the use of *you* and *we*. When he said, "There are two ways you can make boxes," he made it clear that he was aware that other options exist for packaging the toys. He then took on the position of a knowledgeable informer by offering two

April 1997

Dear McDonald's Toy Packagers,

There are two ways you can make boxes for the toys in the Happy Meals so you don't have to have a warning anymore.

The first way is to get a Kleenex box. Then cut out a piece of cardboard from another Kleenex box. Put it over the hole of the first Kleenex box and glue it on. Wrap it up in some paper so it will look nice.

For the second way, you get a shoebox. Then you put paper on it. Cut out one end to put the toy in. Then tape it all up again.

We want kids to be safe and the warning means the bags aren't safe enough. The kids in my class who buy Happy Meals think you should change the bags also.

Gregory

FIG. 6.4.   Gregory's Proposal.

versions of how alternate packaging might be constructed. He did not just name his ideas but outlined how to turn his ideas into reality.

In the final paragraph of his proposal, he evaluated what was currently used as packaging for the toys when he said, "warning means the bags aren't safe enough." What he was saying to McDonald's was that a warning is not enough; you need to do something that is safe for children so that these warning labels are no longer necessary. Finally, Gregory made use of what he knew regarding the role that consumers play in the business market by making it clear that the people involved with submitting the proposal were McDonald's customers.

What Gregory and his "Design a Toy Container" group did was to take the McDonald's toy bags, treat them seriously as classroom text by analyzing them and then constructing new versions. Writing the proposal letter moved them beyond mere interrogation or finding fault (O'Brien, 1998) toward taking action to change, in this case, a specific danger to young consumers.

To represent the McDonald's issues on our audit trail (Fig. 6.5), the children decided to post a Happy Meal bag and a Beanie Baby as artifacts. We also included a receipt and three quotes of topics that came up during our conversations to remind us of those conversations.

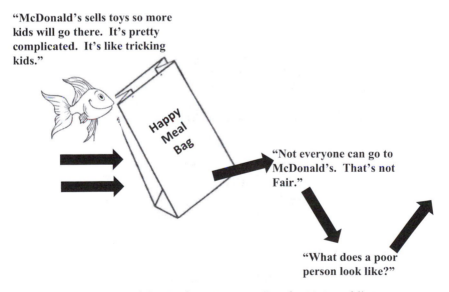

FIG. 6.5. Some of the Artifacts Representing the McDonald's Issue on the Audit Trail.

Critical Reflections and Pedagogical Suggestions

In retrospect, a closer look at the webs the children produced in Figure 6.1, Figure 6.2, and Figure 6.3 brings to the fore an important element that I neglected to explore with them—the human lives behind the production of each item listed on the three webs. Obviously, things do not just come to be. But how often do we think about the host of people behind the production of each food wrapper or Happy Meal toy? Economists might talk in terms of human labor, while sociologists might talk in terms of cultural and/or social capital. Clearly the production of anything in market economies involves a complex network of cultural and human capital. What might we do with our students to take up this issue? One way is to explore more closely the relationship between buyers, sellers, and producers and to talk more extensively about resources, including human resources.

Revisiting the Happy Meal

One of the things we could have done to get at the notion of human labor or cultural capital is to read the Happy Meal box more closely. Following is an example of what I might have done:

- Give each child a bunch of mini dot stickers or any small stickers.
- Pass around the Happy Meal box and have each child place a sticker over one thing they notice.
- When you think you there are no more things to be noticed, begin peeling off each sticker and make a list on chart paper of each item noticed by the children.
- While going over the list, talk about who might want that item or that information. To whom would it be useful? Where might that information be from? Who might have had a hand in adding that information?
- You could then talk about what difference each piece of information might have and for whom it would matter.
- Talk about how the bits of information work to affect/influence you in some way.

This initial activity creates a space for you and your students to begin exploring the relationship between buyers and sellers. This also gets at the idea that the Happy Meal box is a text that is socially constructed and that there is nothing natural or neutral about how it has been put together. Following this, I might have moved to explore the production of the different items in the box.

Taking an item from the box (toy or food item), look closely at the list of ingredients or materials. You could then do the following:

- On chart paper or poster board, make a list of all the ingredients or materials used to make the item you are unpacking.
- Talk about where the materials and ingredients were grown or produced. How might you find out where each item was grown or produced? Who would have had a hand in growing or producing each item?
- How have these items ended up in a Happy Meal box? How were the ingredients or materials transported to the factories where the item might have been made? Did it arrive by airplane, or did it get transported by a truck, ship, or train?
- What are the effects of such transportation on the environment?
- Make a list of all the possible people and groups who may have had a hand in producing the item you are unpacking.
- Talk about how much the particular item might cost and discuss how that item could have been sold for so little given how many people had a hand in its production.

Doing this kind of work may seem daunting or overly challenging, but with the plethora of resources, including videos and other texts, there is so much that we can draw from to help our student learn about just about anything for which they are passionate.

7

A Look Back Over the Year

Organizing a Junior Kindergarten Conference: A Culminating Experience for Our Negotiated Critical Literacy Curriculum

As the end of the school year approached, Melanie arrived in class talking about a conference that her mother had attended. Her enthusiasm was infectious. Other children began asking her questions about the conference. She shared that her mother had listened to different speakers and that she had to sign up to hear them. She also talked about how her mother wore a badge and that there was a book (program) about what was happening at the conference. One of the children asked, "Why did she want to go?" Melanie replied, "To learn."

After several more minutes of conversation about conferences, the children started to talk about how we could have speakers too! Why not, I thought to myself. Igoa (1995) wrote about the importance of the "end of the year good-bye" for giving closure together on the year that has passed. I thought the conference idea would be a terrific way to do this.

Later that evening, I began to list the issues that we had dealt with over the course of the year as well as people we could invite to speak on those topics. From here, plans for a "Junior Kindergarten Conference" began. I brought the idea to the children the next morning. They could not wait to get started. First, we decided on several speakers, including a practicing vegetarian and an animal rights activist.

The next thing we did was come up with a theme, a name for our conference. The children came up with suggestions throughout the day and then went home and asked their parents for suggestions also. One suggestion made by a parent was "Celebrating Our Questions." She said that she had been thinking about what was so different between her daughter's experience in Junior Kindergarten in comparison to the experiences that her older children had and decided that the difference had to do with the kinds of "questions about the world" that my students were asking and that they were asking different questions that were important to them. What a powerful insight! I shared what she had said with the children. We agreed . . . "Celebrating Our Questions" was a good name for our conference.

FIG. 7.1.   Conference Registration Chart.

Once we decided on presenters, we created invitations to formally invite them. We also made posters and badges. We then asked some parents to volunteer as organizers and secured rooms in our school for each of the speakers. While the children created drawings for the letters and posters, I took on the responsibility of creating the program booklet. Figures 7.1, 7.2, and 7.3 show some of the things we made for our conference. The graphic we chose was one we found in a graphics program on our computer. The children liked it because they said the person could be "anybody asking important questions."

When we felt confident that everything we needed to run a conference was in place, we sent out invitations to the children's families and to the other Junior Kindergarten students. We also created a registration sign-up chart where people attending the conference could sign up to participate in two sessions. The conference lasted half a day and was a very powerful and pleasurable (Comber, 1999) experience for everyone.

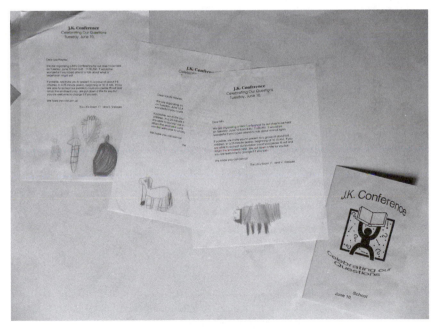

FIG. 7.2.   Letters Inviting Presenters and Conference Booklet.

Presenter Badges

Attendee Badges
The different
colored dots
indicate the session
for which attendees
have registered.

Conference
Program Booklet

FIG. 7.3.   Conference Booklet and Name Badges.

When curriculum is negotiated using the social worlds of children, learning is sustained and generative. Never had I imagined organizing a conference with 3- to 5-year-old children, but the generative nature of our critical literacy curriculum created a space for this kind of complex project to happen. The generativeness comes from providing children opportunities to connect their current understandings with issues that arise in their everyday lives or that of their peers.

Using Social Critique, Social Analysis, and Social Action to Construct Literacy

Throughout the year, social critique, social analysis, and social action were tools that we used to imagine that the social world could be otherwise. We also used these tools to reimagine our world and change the way things were. Through social critique, we began to question why things are the way they are. Through social analysis, we began to look at broad relations and issues of power and control in our community and in society. Through social action, we acted on our critique and analysis reflexively to position ourselves differently so that we may participate in the world in new ways. For example, issues like the vegetarian issue or the French Café issue contributed to change in particular school conditions. As such, some of our actions resulted in a more socially just and equitable community for us to be in. These kinds of actions, if taken on by more teachers in classrooms across the nation, could "quite productively lead to strategies for . . . rebuilding institutions" (Luke et al., 1996, p. 15).

Asking Questions That Matter: A Final Reflection

As a classroom community, we used and constructed our audit trail as a visual representation of our critical literacy curriculum. Our trail became a mediating site through which we began to question traditional social systems in place at our school. In so doing, we began to question the way things were done in our school that did not treat members of our school community in an equitable way.

At the close of our Junior Kindergarten Conference, Lina, a parent of one of the children in the class, approached me and said, "Vivian, the difference between what happened this year, in your classroom, and what happens in some other places is that these children ask questions that matter." Children who learn using curriculum that is based on what matters to them are more likely to feel that what they are learning is important to their lives. This was certainly true in the classroom I shared with my sixteen 3- to 5-year-old students. How might you use the stories of critical literacy learning in our classroom to inform your teaching and to help you make significant the issues and questions that matter to your students? At the time that the first edition of this book was published, I had begun to ask myself similar questions with regard to my work with preservice and inservice teachers and in my work with young children exploring the use of technology and popular culture texts. Since that time, together with my colleagues Jerry Harste and Stacie Tate, we have published the book *Negotiating Critical Literacies with Pre-Service and In-Service Teachers*. I have also coauthored the book *Technology and Critical Literacy in Early Childhood* with Carol Felderman.

What might be your first steps for negotiating the critical issues and questions that matter to your students? How might you create spaces for them to be able to reread and rewrite the world toward becoming the literate people they want and need to be in the new millennium?

During our last class meeting, we sat in a circle so we could see each other. One by one, we reminisced about different instances of living and learning in our classroom. It was hard to believe this was our last class meeting. We had come so far, but we could see how much more we could do and so, as one final experience together, we created a list—"What next year's Junior Kindergartens should know." To bring closure to your experience with this book, I now leave you with our list.

What Next Year's Junior Kindergartens Should Know

- Listen to other kids.
- Remember other people's feelings.
- If there's something happening in the school and you want to go, you can make something like petitions.
- Boys and girls should share their feelings and not fight.
- You have to share with other kids.
- Put things away after you use them.
- You can be strong from your brain.

Epilogue

Why Critical Literacy Continues to Matter Today and in the Future

Over the years, there have been growing accounts of critical literacy work in classrooms (Comber, 2001; Morgan, 1997; O'Brien,

2001; Vasquez, 1994, 1999, 2001, 2005; Vasquez & Egawa, 2003) and more recently accounts of critical literacy in settings outside of the academic year (Kuby, 2013; Vasquez & Felderman, 2013a). Nevertheless, Comber (2013) notes, "critical literacy, with its focus on power and language, has not been a force in early childhood literacy education. Indeed critical literacy is often seen as most appropriate for older or more advanced students" (p. 588). As such, more work needs to be done in order to make available further narratives of critical literacy in practice. Comber, Nixon, and Reid (2007) note that in the teaching of literacy, our role as teachers includes extending the repertoires of literacy and communications practices available to our students. They talk about a pedagogy of responsibility, which they state involves "classroom practice that is informed and structured by teachers' commitment to engaging with questions of diversity and democracy" (p. 14) with their students. Place-based pedagogies, they say, foreground the local and the known and are opportunities for teachers "to structure learning and communication experiences around the things that are most meaningful to their students: their own places, people and popular cultures, and concerns" (p. 14). How then might we provide new, interesting, and different ways for children to communicate their ideas, questions, and understanding about the world around them from a critical literacy perspective and in doing so extend our students repertoire of literacy and communications practices?

While writing about the future of critical literacy, Janks (2010) suggests, "in a world where the only thing that is certain, apart from death and taxes, is change itself critical literacy has to be nimble enough to change as the situation changes" (p. 203). Since the original publication of this book, one of the things that has changed and impacted critical literacy is the increasingly widespread use of technology. In fact, changes in the communicative terrain have made it very difficult to "imagine what the landscape will look like by the time the generation currently in school will graduate" (Janks & Vasquez, 2011, p. 1–6). This is especially true given the speed with which new communication technologies are being developed. It seems like not too long ago when I excitedly had my students sit in front of a computer to sign in for attendance on a black screen with white font. Unfortunately, "where in some homes very young children are able to manipulate and create texts for touch screen smart phones, participate in massively multiplayer online games such as, [*Minecraft*], and play interactive games on computers, others remain without food, shelter, running water, and electricity" (Janks &

Vasquez, 2011, pp. 1–6). In some ways, connectivity has become a class marker, and social differences produce differential access to the world so that the world is more accessible to some than to others. On the one hand, we need to find ways to make the technology accessible to more children. On the other hand, we need to find ways to accept the challenge(s) of the new technological world in which we live to best support children, who participate in the world with new mindsets, identities, and practices that impact their lives at home, at school, and beyond.

New Lenses Through Which to Do Critical Literacy: The Use of Technology

One way of taking on the challenge is to begin to find new lenses through which to do our critical literacy work. One such lens is through the use of technology. Children today are born into a world where technology, such as sending a message or text using a cell phone, creating a video, and participating in online spaces such as electronic art galleries for children, have increasingly become widespread. Figure 7.4 is an image of my two nieces. Hannah is 4 and Elizabeth is 2. The photo was taken shortly after they were given the iPod Touches they are holding in their hands. I was particularly intrigued with the 2-year-old because of the ease with which she navigated the Touch. As soon as she had it in her hand, she turned it on, swiped and tapped the screen, and then held it in the air in the direction of her mom asking "music on?" She was asking for help with using the volume controls and the mute function. Already she understood this technology as a site for participatory learning where she, her sister, and mom would explore entertainment and learning opportunities using the hardware. This kind of interest in technology was evident in work that I did with my colleague Carol Felderman (Vasquez & Felderman, 2013a). We spent some time exploring at the intersection of critical literacy and technology with young children. We were thrilled to learn of new spaces in which early childhood teachers have begun to explore such possibilities. In the book, we share accounts of critical work done with the use of such software as VoiceThread, Tagxedo, and social networking tools such as podcasting. While considering such technologically grounded critical literacy practices, Janks and I (Janks & Vasquez, 2011) argue that new communication landscapes allow for different forms of knowledge production and provide further impetus for critical literacy researchers and teachers to reconsider text production as a source for meaning making.

FIG. 7.4.   Hannah and Elizabeth.

The last bullet in the tenets previously listed, which states that text design and production can provide opportunities for critique and transformation, is really where new technologies and social media could have a strong role. Text design and production refer to the creation or construction of texts and the decisions that are part of that process. This includes the notion that it is not sufficient to simply create texts for the sake of practicing a skill. If children are to create texts, they ought to be able to let those texts do the work intended. For instance, if children are writing surveys or creating petitions, they ought to be done with real-life intent for the purpose of dealing with a real issue. If children write petitions, they ought to be able to send them to whomever they were intended for (Vasquez & Felderman, 2013a). Helping children understand real-life functions of text is an important component of growing as a critically literate individual (Luke & Freebody, 1999; Vasquez, 2005).

However, I want to be clear that the use of new technologies and social media does not constitute engagement with critical literacies. Just because one is using new technology in the classroom, it does not mean they are simultaneously engaging in critical literacies. These new technologies and social media can be used as tools to carry out our critical literacy work by helping us to think and make meaning differently. Such tools can be used to think differently about texts, in the production of texts, and also in the distribution of texts both locally and globally.

Appendix A

Resources for Negotiating Critical Literacies

Boran, S., & Comber, B. (Eds.). (2001). *Critiquing whole language and classroom inquiry.* Urbana, IL: NCTE.

Bourdieu, P. (1991). *Language and symbolic power.* G. Raymond & M. Adamson, Trans. Cambridge, England: Polity Press.

Comber, B. (2009). Critical literacies in place: Teachers who work for just and sustainable communities. In J. Lavia & M. Moore (Eds.), *Cross-cultural perspectives on policy and practice: Decolonizing community contexts* (pp. 43–57). Mahwah, NJ: Taylor & Francis.

Comber, B., & Nixon, H. (2008). Spatial literacies, design texts, and emergent pedagogies in purposeful literacy curriculum. *Pedagogies: An International Journal, 3*(4), 221–240.

Comber, B., & Simpson, A. (Eds.). (2001). *Negotiating critical literacies in classrooms.* Mahwah, NJ: Lawrence Erlbaum Associates.

Davies, B. (1993). *Shards of glass: Children reading and writing beyond gendered identities.* NSW, Australia: Allen & Unwin.

Edelsky, C. (Ed.). (1999). *Making justice our project.* Urbana, IL: NCTE.

Gee, J. P. (1996). *Social linguistics and literacies: Ideology in discourse.* Philadelphia, PA: The Falmer Press.

Gee, J. P. (1999). *An introduction to discourse analysis.* New York, NY: Routledge.

Janks, H. (2009). *Literacy and power.* New York, NY: Routledge.

Janks, H., Dixon, K., Ferreira, A., & Granville, S. (2014). *Doing critical literacy: Texts and activities for students and teachers.* New York, NY: Routledge.

Klein, N. (2001). *No logo: Taking aim at the brand bullies*. Toronto, ON, Canada: Vintage Canada Press.

Lankshear, C., & McLaren, P.L. (Eds.). (1993). *Critical literacy: Politics, praxis, and the postmodern*. Albany: State University of New York Press.

Luke, A., & Freebody, P. (1999). *Further notes on the four resources model. Reading Online*. Retrieved from readingonline.org/research/lukefreebody.html

Marsh, J. (Ed.). (2005). *Popular culture, media and digital literacy in early childhood culture*. London, UK: Falmer Press.

Morgan, W. (1997). *Critical literacy in the classroom*. London, UK: Routledge.

Muspratt, S., Luke, A., & Freebody, P. (Eds.). (1997). *Constructing critical literacies: Teaching and learning textual practice*. Cresskill, NJ: Hampton Press.

Nixon, H., & Comber, B. (2009). Literacy, landscapes and learning in a primary classroom. In M. Somerville, K. Power, & P. de Carteret (Eds.), *Landscapes and learning: Place studies for a global world* (pp. 119–138). The Netherlands: Sense Publishers.

O'Brien, J. (1994). Show mum you love her: Taking a new look at junk mail. *UKRA Reading, 28*(1), 43–46.

Steinberg, S.R., & Kincheloe, J.L. (Eds.). (1997). *Kinder-culture: The corporate construction of childhood*. Boulder, CO: Westview Press.

Vasquez, V. (1994). A step in the dance of critical literacy. *UKRA Reading, 28*(1), 39–43.

Vasquez, V. (2000). Our way: Using the everyday to create a critical literacy curriculum. *Primary Voices, 9*(2), 8–13, Urbana, IL: NCTE.

Vasquez, V. (Ed.). (2001). Critical literacy: What is it and what does it look like in elementary classrooms. *School Talk, 6*(3), Urbana, IL: NCTE.

Vasquez, V. (2010). *Getting beyond "I like the book": Creating spaces for critical literacy across the curriculum*. Newark, DE: IRA.

Vasquez, V., & Felderman, C. (2011). Critical literacy goes digital: Exploring intersections between critical literacies and new technologies with young children. In R. Myers & K. Whitmore (Eds.), *Reclaiming reading*. Mahwah, NJ: Routledge.

Vasquez, V., & Felderman, C. (2013). *Technology and critical literacy in early childhood*. New York, NY: Routledge.

Vasquez, V., Tate, S., & Harste, J.C. (2013). *Negotiating critical literacies with pre-service and in-service teachers*. New York, NY: Routledge.

Appendix B
Alternate Possibilities for Constructing an Audit Trail

Picture Book Illustrations Audit Trail

While teaching third grade, Lee Heffernan had her students read and discuss children's literature with social and political themes. As a way to demonstrate their learning, she had students choose one illustration from the book that they felt captured its essence. She then posted a copy of the illustrations as the artifacts on their learning wall.

Picture Books and Photographs

While creating spaces for critical literacies in her first-grade classroom, Kevan Miller used a combination of photographs of children at work and book covers on their audit trail. The artifacts were posted across the front of the classroom at eye level where the children gathered for whole-group conversations. Thus, the children could readily see and refer back to artifacts representing previous learning experiences.

Artwork Learning Wall

At first, Giorgio Aldighieri, from Toronto, Ontario, Canada, used an audit trail in his French-as-a-second-language classroom as a tool for livening up the space. His classroom was located in the basement of the building with hallways that he described as dark and disconnected from the rest of the school. In an effort to breathe life into the gloomy space, he decided to start an audit trail with his students. The artifacts posted included any artifact of learning, such as the children's artwork. Because he was a French teacher, he worked with several groups of children so that the audit trail he created with his students was not bound by membership in a particular class. Thus, many more individuals were invested in the construction of the audit trail, which made it much more appreciated as it made its way out of the basement and into the staircases and upper hallways. Giorgio even used the ceiling and the gymnasium walls.

By the end of the school year, the audit trail did not only serve a decorative function: It grew to become a sort of touchstone text that all the groups Giorgio worked with could connect with and reflect upon in various spaces throughout the school building.

Wonder Wall

On Twitter, Kristin Zeimke shared her use of what she refers to as a "wonder wall" as an audit trail. Kristin had her young students post what they were wondering about on sticky notes. Refer to Figure B.1 for an illustration of this wall.

I WONDER

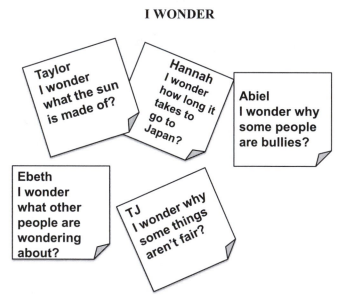

FIG. B.1.   Wonder Wall.

What Might Technology Afford the Construction of an Audit Trail?

The availability of new and/or enhanced technological tools has certainly opened up further possibilities for ways we can create audit trails/learning walls. Technology not only allows us to do various things that we have not done before, but it also allows us to do things differently. Therefore, the question is, what can technology afford the work that we do?

Podcast as Audit Trail

Carol Felderman and I worked with her second-grade students on podcasting. A podcast is an on-demand Internet broadcast that is subscribable. What this means is that listeners can subscribe to the podcast so that their playlist is updated whenever a new show is released. The show we did with the second graders was called *100% Kids* because the topics the children talked about on each episode stemmed from their ideas, questions, and interests. *100% Kids* focused on sharing the children's attempts at contributing to change inequitable ways of being in their school community and beyond. The collection of podcast episodes, of which there were ten, serve as an audio Internet audit trail of learning and thinking. To listen to the children's podcast, go to www.bazmakaz.com/100kids/. Figure B.2 is a visual of the different episodes that served as audio artifacts posted in a virtual space.

PowerPoint or Keynote Learning Walls

Using Power Point (available at www. Microsoftstore.com) or Keynote (available at www.apple.com/iwork/keynote/), audit trails can be created and stored in either a virtual space or printed out and posted on a wall or in the hallway.

Multimodal Audit Trails Using VoiceThread

A VoiceThread (available at voicethread.com is a collaborative, multimedia slide show that can be used to create a multimodal audit trail. On it, you can post images, documents, and videos. The software also allows viewers to navigate slides and leave comments in five ways—using voice (with a mic or telephone), text, audio file, or video (via a webcam). This means that when you share a

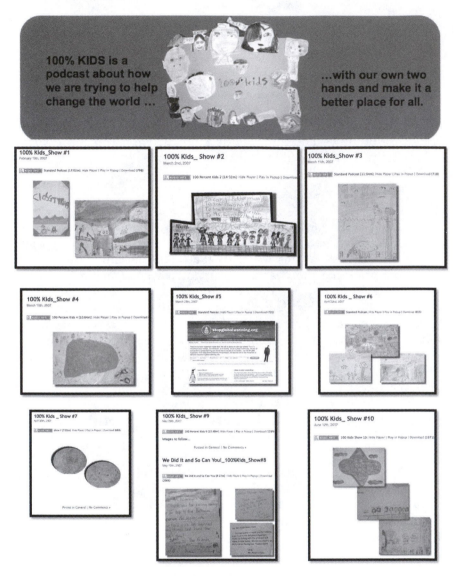

FIG. B.2.   Podcast as Audit Trail.

VoiceThread with friends, family, colleagues, or anyone else, they are able to record comments in audio, video, or text format directly on the image itself. The VoiceThread slides can be made public or kept private.

Audit Trail as a Virtual World

At the time of this writing, I was exploring the possibility of using electronic sandbox games such as *Minecraft* in educational settings, as tools for creating audit trails of learning. A sandbox game is a type of game in which there are minimal character limitations placed on the gamer. This means that the person playing the game can roam around a virtual world adapting and changing that world and the characters within that world. Thus, in a sandbox game, players can roam freely in a virtual space while building and creating.

Minecraft is a sandbox game about mining for bricks and other items and then using those bricks and items to craft or build things. In the beginning, people built structures to protect against monsters such as creepers, but as the game grew, players began creating not only imaginative figures, but imaginative worlds as well. Modifications to the game, known as *Minecraft Mods*, began to emerge. At the time of this writing, there were over 64,000 discussions regarding Mods being developed or talked about by gamers or those interested in *Minecraft* (forum available at www.minecraftforum.net/forum/51-minecraft-mods/). According to the company's website, since 2009, the game has been purchased by over 11,166,590 people as of July 4, 2013 ("*Minecraft* Statistics," 2013).

I am particularly interested in exploring how children and teachers together might create audit trails of learning in a *Minecraft* space. What might a virtual world audit trail of learning look and sound like? Perhaps each instance being represented on the trail can be located in a virtual building or structure that readers can venture into. This means the person creating the audit trail could build multidimensional artifacts to represent his or her learning. Viewers would not only read or listen to particular artifacts, but also interact with them virtually. Each building could have a character that talks about a particular instance of learning being represented. For example, Figure B.3 is a screenshot of a town my 8-year-old son was working on in *Minecraft*. Each of the structures in the image could hold artifacts (also created virtually) representing literacy events or projects that children are working on or have completed. Or perhaps instead of individual structures, one might build a virtual house in which each room represents artifacts of learning about a particular topic or event. Another possibility is to build artifacts across the virtual world where the viewer might take a train or car or some other vehicle to reach each artifact and interact with it.

FIG. B.3.   *Minecraft* Virtual Audit Trail.

The possibilities are endless and I cannot wait to see what might be done with this idea in the near future. For more information on *Minecraft*, visit minecraft.net.

Arts-Based Audit Trails

Audit trails don't have to be put up on a wall or organized in a virtual space. Other options include creating a series of 3-dimensional dioramas or creating sculptures that represent moments in time. The key is that whatever is created needs to be available for revisiting and future reflection. It has to be accessible so that learners can engage in ongoing connecting and reconnecting of learning and thinking over time.

References

Baker, J. (1988). *Where the forest meets the sea.* New York: Harper Collins.

Bigelow, B., Christensen, L., Karp, S., Miner, B., & Peterson, B. (Eds.). (1994). *Rethinking our classrooms: Teaching for equity and justice.* Milwaukee, WI: Rethinking Schools.

Bourdieu, P. (1991). *Language and symbolic power.* G. Raymond & M. Adamson, Trans. Cambridge, England: Polity Press.

Bourdieu, P. (1993). *The fields of cultural production.* Cambridge, England: Polity Press.

Burke, C. (1998, February). Invitations. Seminar presented at Indiana University, Bloomington.

Caldwell, L. (1997). *Bringing Reggio Emilia home: An innovative approach to early childhood education.* New York, NY: Teachers College Press.

Comber, B. (1999, November). Critical literacies: Negotiating powerful and pleasurable curricula—How do we foster critical literacy through English language arts? Paper presented at National Council of Teachers of English Annual Convention, Denver.

Comber, B. (2001). Negotiating critical literacies. *School Talk, 6*(3),1–2. Urbana, IL: National Council of Teachers of English.

Comber, B. (2013). Critical literacy in the early years: Emergence and sustenance in an age of accountability. In J. Larson & J. Marsh (Eds.), *Handbook of research in early childhood literacy* (2nd ed., pp. 587–601). London, UK: Sage/Paul Chapman.

Comber, B., & Cormack, P. (1997, November). Looking beyond skills and processes: Literacy as social and cultural practices in classrooms. *UKRA Reading.*

Comber, B., & Kamler, B. (1997). Critical literacies: Politicizing the language classroom. *Interpretations, 30*(1), 30–53.

Comber, B., Nixon, H., & Reid, J. (Eds.). (2007). *Literacies in place: Teaching environmental communications.* Newtown, NSW, Australia: Primary English Teachers Association.

Comber, B., & Simpson, A. (Eds.). (2001). *Negotiating critical literacies in classrooms.* Mahwah, NJ: Lawrence Erlbaum Associates.

Common Core State Standards Initiative. (2012). Retrieved from http://www.corestandards.org/ELA-Literacy/SL/K

Cordeiro, P. (Ed.) (1995). *Endless possibilities.* Portsmouth, NH: Heinemann.

Dyson, A. H. (1993). *Social worlds of children learning to write.* New York: Teachers College Press.

Fiske, J. (1989). *Reading the popular.* London: Routledge Press.

Forman, G., & Gandini, L. (Producers). (1997). *An amusement park for birds: Documentation of a long-term project from Reggio Emilia* [DVD Reggio Emilia]. Italy: Reggio Children Publisher.

Fox, M. (1993). *Radical reflections.* Fort Washington, PA: Harvest Books.

Frank, B. (2008, July 7). Paper presented at the Literacies and Differences Workshop, Mississauga, ON, Canada.

Freebody, P., & Luke, A. (1990). "Literacies" programs: Debates and demands in cultural context. *Prospect: The Australian Journal of TESOL, 5*(3), 7–16.

Freire, P., & Macedo, D. (1987). *Literacy: Reading the word and the world.* South Hadley, MA: Bergin & Garvey.

Gee, J. P. (1999). *An introduction to discourse analysis theory and method* (2nd ed.). New York, NY: Routledge.

Genishi, C., & Haas Dyson, A. (2009). *Children language and literacy: Diverse learners in diverse times.* New York, NY: Teachers College Press.

Guidici, C., Rinaldi, C., & Krechevsky, M. (Eds.) (2001). *Making learning visible: Children as individual and group learners.* Cambridge, MA: Project Zero, Harvard Graduate School of Education.

Goodman, Y. M., Watson, D. J. & Burke, C. (1987). *Reading miscue inventory: Alternative procedures.* Katonah, NY: Richard C. Owen Publishers.

Harste, J., Short, K. G. & Burke, C. (1996). *Creating classrooms for authors and inquirers* (2nd edition). Portsmouth, NH: Heinemann.

Harste, J., & Vasquez, V. (1998). The work we do: Journal as audit trail. *Language Arts, 75*(4), 266–276.

Harste, J., Woodward, V., Burke, C. (1984). *Language Stories and Literacy Lessons.* Portsmouth, NH: Heinemann.

Hendrick, J. (Ed.). (1997). *First steps toward teaching the Reggio way.* Upper Saddle River, NJ: Prentice Hall.

Horovitz, B. (1999, February 8). McDonald's Furby: Will it flourish or flop? *USA Today,* p. O3.B.

hooks, b. (1994). *Teaching to transgress: Education as the practice of freedom.* New York, NY: Teachers College Press.

Igoa, C. (1995). *The inner world of the immigrant child.* Mahwah, NJ: Lawrence Erlbaum.

Janks, H. (1993). *Language, identity, and power.* Johannesburg, South Africa: Witwatersrand University Press.

Janks, H. (2010). *Literacy and power.* New York, NY: Routledge.

Janks, H. & Vasquez, V. (2011, May). Critical literacy revisited: Writing as critique. *English Teaching: Practice and Critique, 10*(1), 1–6.

Johnston, P. (2004). *Choice words.* Portland, ME: Stenhouse.

Kamler, B. (1994). Resisting oppositions in writing pedagogy or what process genre debate? *Idiom, 29*(2), 14–19.

Klein, N. (2001). *No logo: Taking aim at the brand bullies.* Toronto, ON, Canada: Vintage Canada Press.

Kuby, C. (2013). *Critical literacy in the early childhood classroom: Unpacking histories, unlearning privilege.* New York, NY: Teacher's College Press.

Larson, J., & Marsh, J. (2005). *Making literacy our project.* New York, NY: Routledge.

Luke, A., Comber, B., & O'Brien, J. (1996). Critical literacies and cultural studies. In G. Bull & M. Anstey (Eds.), *The literacy lexicon* (pp. 1–18). Melbourne, Australia: Prentice-Hall.

Luke, A., & Freebody, P. (1999). Further notes on the four resources model. *Reading Online.* Retrieved from readingonline.org/research/lukefreebody.html

Luke, A. & Freebody, P. (2003) Literacy as engaging with new forms of life: The four roles model. In G. Bull & M. Anstey (Eds.) *The literacy lexicon.* Prentice Hall, Sydney, Australia.

Luke, C. (1997). Media literacy and cultural studies. In S. Muspratt, A. Luke, & P. Freebody (Eds.), *Constructing critical literacies: Teaching and learning textual practice* (pp. 19–49). Cresskill, NJ: Hampton Press.

Maras, L., & Brummett, W. (1995). Time for change: Presidential elections in a grade 3–4 multi-age classroom. In P. Cordeiro (Ed.), *Endless possibilities* (pp. 89–104). Portsmouth, NH: Heinemann.

Marsh, J. (Ed.). (2005). *Popular culture, media and digital literacy in early childhood culture.* London, UK: Falmer Press.

McCourt, F. (1996). *Angela's ashes.* Interview at the University of Notre Dame.

Meacham, S.J. (2003, March). Literacy and street credibility: Plantations, prisons, and African American literacy from Frederick Douglass to Fifty Cent. Presentation at the Economic and Social Research Council Seminar Series Conference, Sheffield, United Kingdom.

Minecraft statistics. (2013). Retrieved July 4, 2013, from https://minecraft.net/stats

Morgan, W. (1997). *Critical literacy in the classroom: The art of the possible.* New York, NY: Routledge.

Murphy, S. (2003). Finding literacy: A review of the research on literacy assessment in early childhood education. In N. Hall, J. Larson, & J. Marsh (Eds.), *Handbook of early childhood literacy* (pp. 369–378). London, UK: Sage.

O'Brien, J. (1994). Show mum you love her: Taking a new look at junk mail. *UKRA Reading, 28*(1), 43–46.

O'Brien, J. (1998). Experts in Smurfland. In M. Knobel & A. Healy (Eds.), *Literacies in the primary classroom.* Newton, New South Wales: Primary English Teaching Association.

O'Brien, J. (2001). Children reading critically. A local history. In B. Comber & A. Simpson (Eds.), *Critical literacy at elementary sites* (pp. 37–54). Mahwah, NJ: Lawrence Erlbaum Associates.

Pahl, K., & Rowsell, J. (2010). *Artifactual literacies: Every object tells a story.* New York, NY: Teachers College Press.

Raffi. (1992). *Baby Beluga.* Toronto, Canada: Crown Publishers.

Rinaldi, C. (2004). Documentation and assessment: What is the relationship? *Innovations, 11*(1), 1–4. Detroit, MI: The Merrill-Palmer Institute, Wayne State University.

Stephens, D. (1999). *Assessment as inquiry: Learning the hypothesis-test process.* Urbana, IL: NCTE.

Vasquez, V. (1994). A step in the dance of critical literacy. *UKRA Reading, 28*(1), 39–43.

Vasquez, V. (1998). Building equitable communities: Taking social action in a kindergarten classroom. *Talking Points, 9*(2), 3–7

Vasquez, V. (1999). *Negotiating critical literacies with young children.* Unpublished doctoral dissertation, Indiana University, Bloomington.

Vasquez, V. (2000a). Building community through social action. *School Talk, 5*(4), 2–4.

Vasquez, V. (2000b). Language stories and critical literacy lessons. *Talking Points, 11*(2), 5–8.

Vasquez, V. (2000c). Our way: Using the everyday to create a critical literacy curriculum. *Primary Voices, 9*(2), 8–13.

Vasquez, V. (2001). Constructing a critical curriculum with young children. In B. Comber & A. Simpson (Eds.), *Critical literacy at elementary sites* (pp. 55–66). Mahwah, NJ: Lawrence Erlbaum Associates.

Vasquez, V. (2004). *Negotiating critical literacies with young children.* New York, NY: Routledge.

Vasquez, V. (2005). Creating spaces for critical literacy with young children: Using everyday issues and everyday text. In J. Evans (Ed.), *Literacy moves on* (pp. 78–97). Abingdon, UK: David Fulton Publishers.

Vasquez, V., & Egawa, K. (2003). *Critical literacy: Putting a critical edge on your teaching focused study.* Urbana, IL: National Council of Teachers of English.

Vasquez, V., & Felderman, C. (2007, June 20). *One hundred percent kids podcast.* Retrieved from http://www.bazmakaz.com/100kids/

Vasquez, V., & Felderman, C. (2013a). *Technology and critical literacy in early childhood.* New York, NY: Routledge.

Vasquez, V., & Felderman, C. (2013b). What's new in critical literacy? In K. Wood, J. Paratore, B. Kissel, & R. McCormack (Eds.), *International Reading Association's What's new series.* Newark, DE: International Reading Association.

Vasquez, V., Tate, S., & Harste, J. C. (2013). *Negotiating critical literacies with teachers*. New York, NY: Routledge.

Wohlwend, K. (2011). *Playing their way into literacies*. New York: TC Press.

Wood, D., & Wood, A. (1993). *Quick as a cricket*. Toronto, ON: Child's Play.

Zeimke, K. (2013, June 28). Our wonder wall is constantly changing as kids investigate new wonders and find the answers [Twitter]. Retrieved from https://twitter.com/1stgradethinks/status/361652500144726017/photo/1

Author Index

Subject Index

Permissions

Cover illustration from *Baby Beluga* by Raffi, illustrated by Ashley Wolff. Illustrations copyright © 1990 by Ashley Wolff. Shown on pages 54, 94, 137, 142.

Book cover from *Bad Egg: The True Story of Humpty Dumpty* by S. Hayes (1992). Copyright © 1992 by Little, Brown and Company. Reprinted with permission. Shown on pages 46 and 87.

Inside book cover from *Crafty Chameleon* by M. Hadithi (1989). Copyright © 1989 by Hodder and Stoughton Publishers. Shown on page 96.

Book cover from *The Great Kapok Tree* by L. Cherry (1990). Copyright © 1990 by Harcourt Inc. Reprinted with permission. Shown on pages 46 and 87.

Inside cover from *Panther Dream* by B. Weir (1993). Copyright © 1993 by Hyperion. Shown on pages 52 and 92.

Cover from *Rain Forests* by J. Wood (1993). Copyright © 1993 by Barrons. Shown on pages 39 and 81.

Cover and illustration from page 1, from *Something from Nothing* by Phoebe Gilman. Copyright © 1992 by Phoebe Gilman. Shown on pages 44 and 84.

Book cover from *Where the Forest Meets the Sea* by J. Baker (1988). Copyright © 1988 by HarperCollins. Used by permission of Harper Collins Publishers. Shown on pages 43, 84, and 132.

Illustration from *Where the Forest Meets the Sea* by J. Baker (1988). Copyright © 1988 by HarperCollins. Used by permission of Harper Collins Publishers. Shown on pages 44, 65, and 85.

Two illustrations from *Why the Willow Weeps* by Marshall Izen. Copyright ©1992 by Marshall Izen & Jim West. Shown on pages 50 and 90.

Cover from *Window* by Jeannie Baker (1991). Copyright © 1991 by Penguin Books Canada. Shown on pages 46 and 87.

Book cover from *Quick As a Cricket* by Audrey Wood, illustrated by Don Wood (1993). Copyright © 1982 by M. Twinn. Used with permission from Child's Play (International), Ltd., c 2003. Shown on pages 35, 39, and 81.

Image from *Quick As a Cricket* by Audrey Wood, illustrated by Don Wood (1993). Copyright © 1982 by M. Twinn. Used with permission from Child's Play (International), Ltd., c 2003. Shown on pages 34 and 81.

Text extract from *Quick As a Cricket* by Audrey Wood, illustrated by Don Wood (1993). Copyright © 1982 by M. Twinn. Used with permission from Child's Play (International), Ltd., c 2003. Shown on page 33.

Figure 1.3 is adapted from Manning's "Recursive Cycle of Learning." From A. Manning (1999), *Foundations of Literacy Course Book*. Adapted with permission. Shown on page 18.

All efforts have been made to obtain permission for copyrighted materials, including no less than two written requests to the copyright holder.